Dear Ann,
Dear Mary

A Correspondence
of Grief and Friendship

by

Ann Carli and Mary Woods Scherr

Peace & Love,
Mary

Cover and interior design by Teri Rider.
Photos by Roxyanne Young Photography.

Permissions

We gratefully acknowledge permission to reprint the previously published material.

Excerpts from "An Evening Prayer for the Sabbath" and "When I Lose Myself in Thee" by Tukaram from *God Makes the Rivers to Flow, An Anthology of the World's Sacred Poetry and Prose*, by Eknath Easwaran, founder of the Blue Mountain Center of Meditation, copyright 2003, 2009; reprinted by permission of Nilgiri Press, P.O. Box 256, Tomales, California 94971. www.easwaran.org.

"Farewell Sweet Dust" from *The Collected Poems of Elinor Wylie* by Elinor Wylie, copyright 1932 by Alfred A. Knopf, a division of Random House, Inc., copyright renewed 1969 by Edwina C. Rubenstein. Used by permission of Alfred A. Knopf, a division of Random House, Inc. Any third party use of this material, outside of this publication, is prohibited. Interested parties must apply directly to Random House, Inc. for permission.

"Stop All The Clocks," copyright 1940 and renewed 1968 by W. H. Auden, from *Collected Poems of W. H. Auden* by W. H. Auden. Used by permission of Random House, Inc. Any third party use of this material, outside of this publication, is prohibited. Interested parties must apply directed to Random House, Inc. for permission.

"To be of use" from *Circles on the Water* by Marge Piercy, copyright 1982 by Middlemarsh, Inc. Used by permission of Alfred A. Knopf, a division of Random House, Inc. Any third party use of this material, outside of this publication, is prohibited. Interested parties must apply directly to Random House, Inc. for permission.

"Wish You Were Here," music and lyrics by Harold Rome, copyright 1952. All rights reserved by family.

In Memory of

Angelo Carli
and
Stuart Norman Scherr

Introduction

*D*ear Ann, Dear Mary is a story of two women who console and support each other through a series of e-mails following the deaths of their husbands. The immediacy of electronic mail elicits unusual candor between Mary, a widow of five years, who has found solace through work and meditation and Ann, who struggles with the recent death of her husband exposing raw emotion and unrelenting frankness. Although they lived only one mile apart, it was the e-mail letters, often written late at night, that created the close bond between them.

The women discuss their journeys of grief, share mystical experiences, confess emotional chasms and sexual yearnings, appreciate their differing philosophies, and come to terms with the bittersweet joys of ongoing life. Their letters trace a growing friendship and reveal the transformative power of shared experiences and reflections.

Their exchange portrays the nature of loving relationships and shows the surprising similarities as well as the differences in their long marriages. Through the passing seasons the women share poetry, prayers, music, creative rituals, and dreams as unexpected memories drift into stream-of-consciousness exchanges.

Beyond the experience of loss, these letters chronicle the survival of the human spirit through nature and art, friendship and humor, creativity and spirituality.

Winter

From: Scherr, Mary
Sent: Fri 1/21/2005 7:37 p.m.
To: ann_carli@yahoo.com
Subject: Thinking of you

Dear Ann,

Oh, how often I think of you and send loving thoughts, warm hugs, and strength. I'd love to serve you breakfast or lunch or dinner or tea or a midnight snack. I'm up late so if you need to talk please, please, call. I so wish there was something I could do.

Pam said Angelo didn't want visitors and I can certainly understand his wish but I am so sorry I didn't see him earlier. I never thought events would move so quickly as I, like you, was holding positive thoughts regarding his treatments; but now I can only send prayers and love to you, Angelo, and your family. If you need a safe place to run to or a place for tears, I am here.

Love, mary

From: Carli, Ann
Sent: Fri 1/21/2005 9:28 p.m.
To: MaryScherr@aol.com
Subject: Re: Thinking of you

Dear Mary, my friend,

Your loving words bring tears to my eyes. I so appreciate your writing. I see the lovely orchid you gave me at Christmas each day and thank you in my mind. Do you hear me?

Life is so difficult right now. I just don't have the energy to talk. All my resources are going to Angelo. I dread when the phone rings because I know it will be someone calling to see how Angelo is and to verbalize the state of affairs over and over is draining. E-mail is such a great gift because I can receive good wishes and write brief summaries of where we are. It also gives me solace to sit alone in the dark and just pour out my heart. At some point I will return to the world and my loving friends who have been so caring during this time. I know you will have much to teach me.

I will close with something Angelo said to me at the Getty Museum in November. We had gone for just an hour on the Sunday before his chemotherapy treatment on Monday. We didn't see much; just sat in the sun and talked. He reflected how teaching literature and the humanities had taught him how to live and prepared him to die. He remarked that often people say that a life-threatening disease enhances their senses—that they appreciate life more—but that wasn't his experience at all. He held my hand and said he had always truly appreciated the world and his life to the fullest. This was one of many treasured moments we have had throughout our forty-three years together.

Love, Ann

From: Scherr, Mary
Sent: Mon 1/24/2005 2:59 p.m.
To: ann_carli@yahoo.com
Subject: Sending Love

Dear Ann,

I was so glad to find your message today when I returned from Seattle. I also had a phone message update from Pam, who has been a dear in keeping me informed.

I completely understand how draining you find phone calls and questions from concerned friends. When Stu was hospitalized with his first heart attack and I was going back and forth all day long, I remember hoping that I could drive into my garage and close the door before neighbors came out to find out what was happening. I yearned for complete privacy, and I found it hard to be even polite although I also knew their questions represented love—but I couldn't handle the responses that I needed to give.

I didn't communicate with friends by e-mail at that time, which would have been much easier, I think.

I am sending you love, warm wishes, and hugs—to you and your family.

What a treasure your relationship with Angelo has been—and how fortunate that he verbalized his appreciation of life during that visit to the Getty last November. Good memories do provide a measure of solace. And someday we'll talk about and cry about both the tragedy and the advantage of knowing when life is ending as opposed to the shock of a sudden death. How I wished that I had expressed more often and more clearly my love, respect, and appreciation. Yet I tried to be grateful that he died exactly as he wished: suddenly without any warning signal.

Please take care of yourself and know that your friends want to help ease your pain in any way that we can.

Love, love, love, mary

From: Carli, Ann
Sent: Sat 1/29/2005 6:50 p.m.
To: MaryScherr@aol.com
Subject: Re: Sending love

Dear Mary,

 We said goodbye to Angelo this afternoon at
12:30 p.m.
 Your loving messages have meant a lot. You and
I have much to talk about. And we will soon.

Love, Ann

From: Scherr, Mary
Sent: Mon 1/31/2005 9:55 p.m.
To: ann_carli@yahoo.com
Subject: Love and warm hugs

Dear, Dear Ann,

I just returned from L.A. and received your e-mail.
Oh, my dear—I didn't realize the end was so near
but I am glad he didn't suffer any longer. And how
wonderful that the entire family was with him for a
final goodbye. That is a special blessing!
Annie said the service was planned for the 12th. I
will do anything that I can.
Would you like Annie and me to do flowers? Or is
there a preference for something else or in addition?

Sending love and warm hugs, mary

From: Carli, Ann
Sent: Tues 2/1/2005 10:39 a.m.
To: MaryScherr@aol.com
Subject: Angelo's obituary

Dear Mary,

   There is a lovely article about Angelo in the
North County Times this morning.

   I think the writer wrote an extraordinary piece,
capturing Angelo's gentle humor, dedication to
teaching, and delights in life.

   I'm not quite sure what we want for flowers for
the Gathering of Family and Friends to remember
Angelo on February 12. I so appreciate your offer.
May I get back to you in a few days?

Love, Ann

Remembering Angelo Carli

English wasn't the first language for Angelo Carli, but it became his career and his passion.

The son of Italian immigrants walked into his Brooklyn kindergarten classroom at age 5 not speaking a word of English. By the time he wrapped up his 34-year career at Palomar College, Carli had taught English and humanities to thousands of students, co-authored an anthology of poetry used as a text at Palomar and other colleges, and earned two Fulbright Fellowships, one to Durham, England.

"He always thought it was amusing that he as an American was teaching English to the English," said Carli's wife of 43 years, Ann.

Carli, who died Saturday at his home at age 67 after a battle with cancer, enjoyed amusing stories. He told hundreds of them to colleagues, outside his office at Palomar.

"He was a funny man," said English professor Barbara Keller. "He brought laughter to the hallways and high standards to the classroom."

Carli began Palomar as a teacher in 1964. He later served as Director of Veterans' Education and later as Dean of Community education. During his time at the college he helped establish Palomar centers at Camp Pendleton, Fallbrook, Pala, Borrego Springs, and Poway.

During his tenure as Director of Veterans'
Education in the years following the Vietnam War from
1972–79, Carli set up an education program on Camp
Pendleton to help active military personnel to complete
requirements for their high school diplomas.

Grants he obtained helped establish Palomar as
having one of the most distinguished programs for
veterans in the country, said Herman Lee, Director of
Enrollment Services, who worked in the office next to
Carli in those days. Some 4,000 plus veterans returning
from Vietnam benefited from his efforts.

Carli's work with veterans was recognized this past
Veterans Day when the college presented him with its
Distinguished Service Award.

"He valued working with Vietnam veterans. At the
service he said that was the project he was most proud of
in his career," said Ann.

A love of reading drove Carli as a youngster.
He always had a book in his hand, giving an early
indication that he wasn't destined to become the
engineer his family expected him to be. He began college
studying engineering at New York University but
switched to English at San Francisco State, where he
received a Master's degree, after meeting his future wife
during a summer visit to San Diego.

Once he began teaching Carli would stress to students
and colleagues alike the importance of continuing to read.
His home was filled with books that he found exploring
thrift shops, antiques stores, and garage sales.

Among the gems he brought home were first edition texts by economists Thomas Malthus and Adam Smith that he sold through an auction house in New York.

"That helped send our kids through college," Ann said.

Not everything he brought home was hidden treasure. Described light-heartedly by his wife as "somewhat of a Sanford and Son junk collector," Carli filled a three-car garage and a storage unit with the stuff he picked up during his travels.

On the road with his wife, Carli would stop at every antique or thrift store he encountered while Ann would wait patiently in the car reading a book.

Carli's other loves were travel, particularly to Italy, cooking, and the ponies. After returning to the classroom he would spend a good part of the summers where the turf meets the surf at the Del Mar Racetrack. He worked for 15 years managing the boxes in the Turf Club, often gently teasing some of the celebrities he encountered.

"When Tim Conway would come in, he'd say, 'Hello Mr. Korman,' referring to Conway's frequent foil, actor Harvey Korman," Ann recalled. "He loved the racing milieu. He loved the excitement of the races."

A gathering of family and friends will be held at 3 p.m. Saturday, December 12 at Eternal Hills Mortuary, 1999 El Camino Real, Oceanside. (Jeff Rank, Staff Writer, North County Times)

From: Scherr, Mary
Sent: Sun 2/13/2005 9:55 p.m.
To: ann_carli@yahoo.com
Subject: Memorial Service

Dear Ann,

The memorial service for Angelo was lovely, honest, and heartwarming. Through memories and anecdotes, the speakers clearly expressed Angelo's personality.

I loved the cherry trees at the front of the room (I learned later they were weeping cherry trees). I felt the service was a wonderful tribute to Angelo in an unusually honest way. No minister presided. So often one does even when the service is for one without a church affiliation. And the music was lovely.

Your anecdotes about Sabrina and Philip humorously illustrated Angelo's creative, sensitive, and bold approach! How did Angelo happen to go to Philip's school?

Love, mary

From: Carli, Ann
Sent: Tues 2/15/2005 10:39 a.m.
To: MaryScherr@aol.com
Subject: Re: Memorial Service

Dear Mary,

Thank you for attending our Gathering of Angelo's Family and Friends on Saturday. Philip, Sabrina, and I worked together on the flowers, the music, the eulogy. The Puccini arias, Yeats poem, and words about his life gave us solace. Did you see his red truck we had parked outside the chapel? We brought it as his "riderless horse."

I didn't know if I would be able to speak but the loving energy in the room helped me to pay tribute to Angelo as an extraordinary father. Not many people knew this side of him and I wanted to tell the two stories from Philip's and Sabrina's childhood that illustrate how gentle, wise, and devoted he was as their father.

In answer to your question about the story I told of Angelo going to Philip's school, I have to give the background. In 1971 we left Carlsbad to spend a year in England while Angelo was on a Fulbright exchange. It was a hard transition for the kids to leave their home for the year in England, find their place as the two little American children in the northeast English school, and then return to suburban California. They both acquired Geordie accents in that year and it wasn't easy assimilating back. In the hot September Philip wanted to wear short pants to school as he did in England. I didn't think anything about it, but at that time Carlsbad boys did not wear short pants. I got a call from school mid-day saying that Philip was in the principal's office very upset from being teased for his short pants. The principal thought it might be best if I brought him some long pants.

I don't know why I just didn't run the pants over to the school but I called Angelo. He told me to wait, he was coming home from work. In twenty minutes he was home, bounding upstairs. When he came down he was wearing shorts and carrying a pair of Philip's long pants. He drove to the school and sat down with Philip, reassuring him that he was the smart one, wearing cool clothing on a hot day. He told him he could choose to change into the long pants he had brought or not. Philip stayed in his shorts. I like to think of the school kids watching six-foot-two Angelo barreling up in his shorts and eight-year-old Philip gathering up his own courage through his father's model.

Now we must all rely on memories.

Love, Ann

From: Scherr, Mary
Sent: Tues 2/22/2005 10:07 a.m.
To: ann_carli@yahoo.com
Subject: Conversation

Dear Ann,

I thoroughly enjoyed our teatime together yesterday. Last evening I had another suggestion. Don't worry about finances or funding the residual trust for several weeks—you have plenty of time. I was working and didn't know how much time it would take and so I started when I was still numb. I went to our attorney and to our CPA and a week later couldn't understand my notes or remember any of the important points. Later it all seemed reasonable instead of esoteric!

Fortunately, a friend whose husband had died several years ago, told me "Don't think you're crazy or senile if you can't remember things—that's the way it is for many of us." I was relieved when finally I could remember most financial details.

Take care of yourself—you seem to know what you need and that's the first important part of getting thru this transition. Advice by assertive, well-intentioned friends is not always helpful.

Much love and warm hugs, and please call when we can meet again. I'd like that.

Love, mary

From: Carli, Ann
Sent: Wed 2/23/2005 8:06 p.m.
To: MaryScherr@aol.com
Subject: Re: addendum to conversation

Dear Mary,

Thank you for your caring and useful
guidance. You were the first person I wanted to
call after Angelo died. I knew you would have
understanding, insight, and practical advice because
we both had marriages of forty years to wonderful
men. I so appreciated sharing your tears for Stu and
mine for Angelo. This is not the bond we would
have sought, widows together, but it is a bond.

I have made a note to call the attorney who
handled our living trust—something I would
not have done without your suggestion. I went to
the post office this morning and certified all the
life insurance papers as you suggested. I have a
preliminary appointment with our tax accountant,
a man who became Angelo's friend over the
years (as so many business associates did); he
has assured me that he will help me through. I
am approaching each task individually and give
myself LOTS of credit for accomplishing anything.

And yes, I know about that forgetting "am-I-
crazy?" feeling. I wrote two thank you notes to a
friend who had sent flowers. When I discovered

this I put one note inside the other. Before I mailed it I received yet another arrangement from this friend, so I created an envelope inside an envelope inside an envelope. I remember our mutual friend Mary R. telling me when my mother died, "you will be forgiven anything at this time so don't worry about mistakes or oversights."

Thank you for the *Power of Now* book, which I will take to the mountains with me, weather permitting. I have the sweet orchid you gave me at Christmas on the dining room table. It is still in bloom on a bed of polished river rocks. I think of you whenever I see it.

One thought keeps haunting me. Where was I in your grief? I feel like such a thoughtless, insensitive person not to have been aware of what you were going through, not to have called you as you have called me just to say hello, not to have communicated more that I care about you and your family—not just at Stu's memorial service but weeks, months, and years after. Because you have such a loving heart, I feel you have not blamed me, but I am remorseful. You are teaching me how to give comfort to others.

Friends have suggested I join a support group. I have considered this but not acted on it. This is such an individual experience, influenced by personality, family history, religion, and philosophy of life. Although I am an extrovert, I am not inclined to join a group. I find writing helpful and one-on-one conversations with friends who have had great losses the closest to comfort. "Bereavement is a darkness impenetrable to the imagination of the unbereaved." Iris Murdoch

Love, Ann

From: Carli, Ann
Sent: Mon 2/28/2005 10:39 a.m.
To: MaryScherr@aol.com
Subject: Time

Dear Mary,

It has now been a month since we said goodbye to Angelo. I find I need time alone and this is hard for people to understand. I appreciate the care and loving.

So much of my life is opaque now. All the colors seem gone and focus and memory are very weak. I do feel the loving care around me and the circle of my family is very important.

Come spring I hope I will be more grounded. Right now I wish I lived in a little village in the mountains of Italy or Greece and could put on my black dress for the rest of my life, maybe go to church every day—or maybe not.

Love, Ann

From: Scherr, Mary
Sent: Sun 3/6/2005 2:22 p.m.
To: ann_carli@yahoo.com
Subject: Response to Iris Murdock Quote

Dear Ann,

We are experiencing a type of bonding, as you said we would never have sought, but I am grateful that we can share this transition time together.

- We both had long, loving marriages.

- We both experienced great sorrow at Christmas time. Stu was unconscious in the Acute Care Unit; Angelo had advanced cancer symptoms.

- We both have supportive children who had loving relationships with their father.

- We both feel the power of poetry to capture deep feelings and to express the mystery of life.

From my experience, Iris Murdoch is only partially right. The depth of bereavement is unknown and unimaginable to the unbereaved, but my unbereaved friends offered support in wonderfully sensitive ways. One colleague arrived with special pastries and a small Italian angel to be my special guardian while Stu was in the Acute Care Unit. Marge arrived with a platter of rosemary chicken. Jackie's entire family took care of us: preparing food, running errands, babysitting grandchildren, typing the memorial program. And, as you know, Annie arrived in the middle of night shortly after the paramedics. Fortunately Janet and Andrew were still living in Glendale at that time and arrived early the next morning. Cynth and family came that day also.

Please do not judge yourself harshly for not knowing what you could not have known and I certainly did not expect you to. You helped considerably with the flowers for the church. Annie's idea of planning and arranging altar flowers was pure genius. (She put the cacophony of colors and baskets in the narthex.) When I sat down in that front pew and saw white orchids, eucalyptus leaves, and willow branches, I felt soothed and even a little relaxed. Beautiful and lovely and wonderfully appropriate for the flute and clarinet music. So thank you for your substantial part in arranging that altar. And thank you also for writing in the guest book: "A service worthy of our dear Stu." That comment meant a lot to me.

Love, mary

From: Carli, Ann
Sent: Mon 3/7/2005 11:47 a.m.
To: MaryScherr@aol.com
Subject: Angelo's Birth Day

Dear Mary,

The array of eucalyptus and orchids with the evocative sound of clarinet will always be my framework for remembering Stu. I'm glad I wrote that simple sentence that day and am touched that you remembered it. Orchids seem to be a continuing theme in our friendship.

In these past weeks I have clung to the beauty of the physical world. I planted the two weeping cherries we had at Angelo's service in front of the house with three white cascade roses. I think of this as Angelo's garden. The area is very tangled, exactly like my life. But I know I can and will bring order to it.

Today was not as difficult as yesterday. I did something out of a resolve that came to me last night about converting this dark energy into something positive. I sent Angelo's sister a flowering azalea with a card remembering Angelo's birthday. He would really like me doing that, comforting her.

I never underestimated nor undervalued Angelo. You know, I called him Mr. Wonderful all our married life, sometimes chiding him about the W being turned upside down to an M for martyr. He almost always put himself second to others. The ONLY times I remember him not doing so was when he got fed up with others' selfishness and deliberately and petulantly did something outrageously out of character.

Anyhow, although I knew his goodness, I really didn't know others did. I knew he was well liked, well regarded and respected, but I didn't know how much he was loved. I also knew how lucky I was. That helps—a little bit. I am holding on to his voice, his guidance, and reassurance. I hope I don't lose it. When Angelo was fighting for his life I said I was holding on. When he died I said I was holding together. Now I am simply holding up. I don't feel together but the pieces are upright.

Mary, this deep sharing is useful to me.

Love, Ann

From: Scherr, Mary
Sent: Thurs 3/10/2005 10:42 p.m.
To: ann_carli@yahoo.com
Subject: Appreciating Angelo

Dear Ann,

Do you have any idea how many women say, "I never appreciated him enough" or "I didn't know how lucky I was"? Is there a tiny bit of solace in the fact that you never undervalued Angelo? I hope so because many women claim they didn't appreciate their husbands enough.

I, too, talk to Stu. And sometimes I get answers to questions in my dreams. I know that psychologists insist we are the authors of our dreams; nevertheless, I prefer to think of my dreams as mysterious and wonderfully helpful.

Your last e-mail exudes strength, my friend. You have been holding together and holding up. And you are upright! That's progress.

Love, mary

From: Carli, Ann
Sent: Fri 3/11/2005 9:15 p.m.
To: MaryScherr@aol.com
Subject: A Story

Dear Mary,

I have been meaning to tell you a true story that has great meaning to me.

Some time ago, before Angelo became ill, I ran across a wrenching poem by W. H. Auden. It took my breath away because Auden expressed the depth of love I felt for Angelo. Little did I know how years later its significance would come crashing in on me.

Two days after Angelo died I sent this poem to a circle of friends I have known for thirty years, a group who meet six or seven times a year to share the trials and joys of life. Each of these five women knew Angelo well.

Stop All the Clocks
W. H. Auden

Stop all the clocks, cut off the telephone,
Prevent the dog from barking with a juicy bone,
Silence the pianos and with muffled drum
Bring out the coffin, let the mourners come.

Let aeroplanes circle moaning overhead
Scribbling on the sky the message He Is Dead,
Put crepe bows round the white necks of the public doves,
Let the traffic policemen wear black cotton gloves.

He was my North, my South, my East and West,
My working week and my Sunday rest,
My noon, my midnight, my talk, my song;
I thought that love would last for ever: I was wrong.

The stars are not wanted now: put out every one;
Pack up the moon and dismantle the sun;
Pour away the ocean and sweep up the wood.
For nothing now can ever come to any good.

Late in the day the medical equipment company came to collect the hospital bed. Sabrina and I had been distracting ourselves by tidying the room when I noticed my electronic clock, the type that always resets itself in power outages and time changes, had stopped. At first I thought the plug had been knocked out in the moving of the bed but no, it was plugged in. The clock had simply stopped. I took the plug out and then put it back in and it came up with the correct time.

Two of the friends I sent the Auden poem to questioned the line "I thought that love would last forever: I was wrong" maintaining that love does last forever. I responded that I believe Auden was referring to love both as a verb for his deep feelings and as a noun, representing his beloved. The poem speaks to me of the bliss of deep love and the illusion that something so exquisite must be infinite, contrasted with the reality of death bringing an unimaginable emptiness. It is such a pain-filled poem, it is probably difficult for many people. It says what I feel, rejecting platitudes, and so is comforting in a strange way.

Love, Ann

From: Scherr, Mary
Sent: Sun 3/13/2005 7:42 p.m.
To: ann_carli@yahoo.com
Subject: Unexplainable happenings

Dear Ann,

Your clock stopping on the day of Angelo's death is remarkable.

In a way the stopping of the clock is a mechanical tribute; everything should not go on just as if nothing important has happened.

In regards to the poem, I hear it as a marvelous tribute to a deep and abiding love as both a noun and a verb. And I understand what you mean when you write that although it is pain-filled it reflects your intense feeling and therefore is more comforting than platitudes that deny your feelings.

I have had several mystical, unexplainable happenings. Two days after Stu's memorial service, I woke up with the first pale hint of dawn. Where was I? Alone in a king-size bed in a beautiful, but strange room. I glanced to my left and saw the flowers I had brought from home—a soft, lovely, soothing arrangement sent from very close friends. Stu had died five days earlier, the day after Christmas. An overwhelming sense of loneliness, sorrow, and disconnection nearly strangled me. My throat tightened, hot tears slid down onto the pillow. How would I ever be able to live without him. Did I want to?

I shifted ever so slightly and saw a candle burning on the patio. My throat relaxed—light and life and hope.

My two grandchildren had lit a memory candle at Stu's memorial service two days previously. Now I was at a desert resort with my two daughters, their husbands and two grandchildren. Close family friends were in nearby rooms with their children and grandchildren. Our families had planned a special three-day vacation a year in advance to celebrate the New Year 2000. But Stu didn't live to celebrate the millennium.

One candle left over from the gathering in the patio the previous night still gave forth light. I cherished its glow in the early dawn. Directly opposite from me a large window framed a mountain peak. One of my Canadian students had explained that a mountain is one of the important symbols for First Nation people. Mountains represent strength. The glow of light was reassuring; I felt the mountain suggested I would both need and receive strength to get through this vacation without Stu.

The day after my return from Palm Springs, I woke up unusually early. I was contented, happy, and relaxed. In a dream Stu had leaned over and kissed me before leaving the bedroom.

A week later, I woke up in the middle of the night, looked at the clock and saw that it was two a.m. I glanced out of the high west window. A bright star was shining. That's Stu's star, I thought. For several weeks before he died, Stu had told me: If you look out the window at two a.m. you'll see a very bright star. I replied that I'd be willing to take his word for it. But that night and for many following nights I awakened at exactly two a.m. and each time saw the bright star.

For several months I felt blessed by the candle, the kiss, and the star.

Love, mary

From: Carli, Ann
Sent: Mon 3/14/2005 5:07 p.m.
To: MaryScherr@aol.com
Subject: Re: Unexplainable happenings

Dear Mary,

I am so moved by these mystical gifts that appeared during the morning and night so shortly after Stu died. Your beautiful account of the candle glowing in the morning light as a beam of hope with the majestic mountain's strength in the background is reflective of your own hopeful spirit and inner strength.

And how very wonderful to dream of Stu's kiss. I am so glad this brought you contentment and peace, your own loving interpretation. Some might have felt sad with his absence but you felt his presence.

Isn't it interesting that we both had experiences with clocks and time? Your waking to see the star, at exactly the time Stu deemed you could, was like a third message. From him? From your heart? Certainly they were gifts of love.

One of my most important life teachers spoke of symbols years ago and I had forgotten this until you wrote of your experiences. He said there are, if we take the time to see, messages around everywhere to guide us.

We need to watch for these to get us through
the dark night, gray dawn, or even the light of day.
Thank you for sharing this.

Love, Ann

From: Scherr, Mary
Sent: Thurs 3/17/2005 4:00 p.m.
To: ann_carli@yahoo.com
Subject: Gift from the sea

Dear Ann,

This morning my friend from Michigan, who rents a condo on our beach for three months every winter, showed me how she finds tiny tree-like treasures in the sand. At the edge of the shore, where the ocean often leaves trails of shells and seaweed, she discovered miniature seaweed trees. I found one today and left it at your door as a special gift from the sea. On the way home, I wrote the following:

> Buried and entangled in seaweed clumps
> Cast upon the shore
> This perfect, tiny tree unseen
> Except by persistent rummagers
> Who believe in myriad gifts from the sea.

Love, mary

From: Carli, Ann
Sent: Thurs 3/17/2005 10:04 p.m.
To: MaryScherr@aol.com
Subject: Your Gift from the Sea

Dear Mary,

Thank you for the tiny, delicate "seaweed tree"
you left at my doorstep today. I remember that you
and Stu walked on the beach each week—wasn't
Thursday your day? I remember you telling me
about this several years ago and was struck by the
commitment, the intimacy, the romance of this
time you both had set aside for each other. I can
well imagine how close you feel to him now as you
walk along the beach collecting small treasures like
the one you gave to me.

In the last weeks of Angelo's life he said to me,
"You know how you always think of your mother
when you see a hummingbird? Think of me when
it rains." This was a paradoxical thought from him.
Although he knew I love the rain and never tire of
it, it made him anxious because we had so much
trouble with leaks in the roof. He told me once in
Italy when it was raining he felt this sudden unease
until he realized the rain on our poorly constructed
roof had conditioned him. It rained the day he died
and for two weeks afterward.

Your tiny poem honors this tiny treasure, expressing your connection to the ocean. I like sharing poetry and quotations that have meaning for us. I hope we can continue.

Love, Ann

From: Scherr, Mary
Sent: Fri 3/18/2005 4:18 p.m.
To: ann_carli@yahoo.com
Subject: Exchange of poems

Dear Ann,

I, too, am enjoying our exchange of poems. I liked your comments about rain.

It brings to mind a framed epigram by T. N. Hahn that is in my study: "The tears I shed yesterday have become rain." It reminds me to live in ways that my tears become nourishing. And thoughts about nourishing remind me of all the ways Stu nourished his family as well as his patients. I recently heard a spiritual leader say that we could attain deep compassion for others by meditation and prayer or by suffering. We both have friends who have suffered from the death of a spouse who do indeed show a depth of compassion.

On my 70th birthday in March, three months after Stu died, Cynth sent me a card that included two long lists entitled: "Gifts from my father" and "Gifts from my mother." A priceless present with specific and humorous reminders of the memories we will always share.

Within hours after Stu entered the Acute Care Unit we knew the chances of his survival were very slim. Cynthia, Janet, and I started to emphasize our gifts—I did not want to become bitter, or obsessed with the fact that his life was too short. I knew and therefore struggled to feel that I had much to be grateful for. He died the way he wanted—suddenly as his father had done. He lived eight and a half years after his first heart attack and walked down the aisle with Janet, saw the birth of two grandchildren, knew Janet was expecting a girl, and fulfilled his desires for music, photography, and botanical garden volunteerism. We knew there were advantages to a sudden, unexpected death, but, oh, how we all wished we could have said goodbye and expressed our deep love.

Do take care, I love these e-mails.

Love, mary

Gifts from My Father
Cynthia Scherr

*An ability to seek and form connections between
    people, places and things.*
My semitic heritage.
Delight in the crisp and crunch of green peppers.
*The flexibility to adapt to my partner's changing life
    goals.*
*Devotion to family and the desire to attend every
    event in which my children play a part.*
The challenge of a new trail on a mountain.
*The knowledge that going to nature will restore my
    soul.*
A desire to continually learn and change.
A love of music, both practice and performance.
Newspaper clipping fever.
*An example of meticulous commitment to my clients
    and my profession.*
A quirky sense of humor.
101 ways to use the word "integrity."
*An appreciation for things botanical—and an itch to
    find out their real names.*
Music as an expression that goes beyond words.
The next generation of brown eyes.

Gifts from My Mother
Cynthia Scherr

The drive to create a sense of community among
extended family and friends.
The continuation of generations of spiritually aware
women.
The Woods ice cream gene.
Openness to anything new.
Tenderness and deep caring for my children.
An ear for the rhythm and moods of the ocean.
A natural teaching ability.
The value of time to write, to be still, and meditate.
Wisdom and the desire to follow a path to maturity.
The magic of poetry.
Spontaneity and a sense of adventure.
An admirable demonstration of how to be a public
servant.
A sense of mystery.
Generosity of spirit and with material goods.
The desire to surround myself with flowers.
A singing voice I can use.
Hair straight as straw.

From: Carli, Ann
Sent: Fri 3/18/2005 7:34 p.m.
To: MaryScherr@aol.com
Subject: Bearings

Dear Mary,

I just realized that your caring dialogue with
me takes you back five years to Stu's death. I get the
sense it is a heart-warming (rather than chilling)
experience for you. I hope this is so. The experience
of your two daughters joining you in his last hours,
numbering your gifts from him and his own life
joys seem to me the perfect observance for a family
saying goodbye to a beloved. I was very moved
by Cynthia's list of "Gifts from My Father" and
"Gifts from My Mother" which she sent to you on
your following birthday. I can't imagine a more
treasured present.

In the last ten days of Angelo's life Philip
and Sabrina were so strong and courageous,
staying with me by his bedside around the
clock. Toward the end, I asked him "Can you see
how valiant your children are?" and he nodded
and whispered "yes." I know I acknowledged
previously to you how fortunate you and I are to
have remarkable children.

A friend wrote recently, asking the inevitable and dreaded question "How are you doing?" She used the term "emotional bearings." To address her question, I looked up bearing/s: One of my diversions is to study a word that appears in my own or other's writing. It inevitably takes me to interesting places.

Bearings. Function: noun

1: the manner in which one bears or comports oneself
2 a: the act, power, or time of bringing forth offspring or fruit
   b: a product of bearing: CROP
3 a: an object, surface, or point that supports
   b: a machine part in which another part (as a journal or pin) turns or slides
4: a figure borne on a heraldic field
5: pressure, thrust
6 a: the situation or horizontal direction of one point with respect to another or to the compass
   b: a determination of position
   c: plural: comprehension of one's position, environment, or situation
   d: relation, connection; also: purport
7: the part of a structural member that rests on its supports

I found the definitions fascinating and all of them relevant. I know I am functioning, i.e., comporting myself, and getting through the days without much productivity other than business affairs. At present I have no compass and feel no great pressure to find one—for a while, at least. I have certainly been supported in many ways and although I appreciate the support, I seem to resist it. Our correspondence, however, has provided new bearings in working through acceptance of my position, environment, situation, connection, and purpose.

Love, Ann

From: Scherr, Mary
Sent: Sun 3/20/2005 9:55 p.m.
To: ann_carli@yahoo.com
Subject: Giving

Dear Ann,

Your analysis of "bearings" reminds me of the suggestion I offered to one of my colleagues. She was on her way to a university committee meeting and expected to see a professor who had recently lost his wife. She had already written him a note, but asked me what I thought would be the best thing to say. I replied: "Just say it is good to see you" or "I've been thinking of you."

I recall that about a month after Stu died, I was feeling sad and sorry for myself one particular morning. Then I remembered a friend who had lost her husband eight months earlier and whose mother died the same day as Stu did. I called and asked her over for dinner. During the evening she told me that a close friend had assured her that she would be able to find her way and have a rewarding life even though it would be very different. And as the evening ended with her profuse appreciation for the dinner invitation, I realized that I had experienced in a deeper way than ever before what the line from St. Francis really meant: "It is in giving that we receive."

We both have been fortunate to have strong support from friends. Although I knew they wanted to help, I did not know how to ask for support. Perhaps I didn't even realize what I needed, but those who had experienced the same kind of loss instinctively knew I needed companionship and comfort with my teary emotions. One friend softly said with sincere concern: "Oh, I don't like to think of you in tears" after I admitted I had had crying jags off and on all day. And, I found that a few friends who knew Stu well didn't mention his name even when the topic seemed to warrant a reference to him. I felt as if they had forgotten about him already. Gradually I realized they were trying to prevent additional sorrow. Dealing with the inevitably sustained sorrow and the finality of death is difficult for all of us.

Love, mary

Spring

From: Carli, Ann
Sent: Mon 3/21/2005 12:45 p.m.
To: MaryScherr@aol.com
Subject: Re: Giving

Dear Mary,

It is difficult for most people to respond to
death and they even avoid the word. Although I
am not comfortable with "passed away" I do use
it sometimes only to soften the startling news that
Angelo died. A friend expressed her difficulty with
the reference to "losing your husband." She said
she wanted to respond, "I didn't misplace him. He
died." Your suggestion to the person who asked
what to say—"It's good to see you"—is exactly right
in my mind.

"How are you?" and "How are you doing?"
are disconcerting to me. I sometimes perversely
wonder "Does she really want to hear 'Horribly!
I am devastated and don't want to get out of bed
in the morning.'" I refuse to be hypocritical so my
responses run from "I am functioning" to "I am
upright" or "I am holding together." We need to
come up with a series of greetings people might
offer instead of "How are you doing?" And maybe
some responses too. A friend who is fighting
cancer has said the same about these phrases. She

also hates "You look GOOD," which has also been said to me.

In spite of this tirade, I do understand this awkwardness in others. They simply do not know. I tend to be hypersensitive to words. I can't bring myself to use the word "comfort." I feel there is no comfort. However, your understanding, insight, and practical advice have cushioned this time for me, and I am profoundly grateful.

I've been thinking about the St. Francis quotation you sent "It is in giving that we receive." It occurs to me that is something that is not reckoned with in death. A lot is said about the loss of sharing but I think the loss of giving is overlooked—the sweet experience of thinking about someone else's needs and delights. "Giving to" is yet another of the infinite number of parts of Angelo's presence that I no longer have. Angelo was never a material guy but he loved food and music. I could always brighten his day by cooking polenta or gnocchi, foods of his childhood and family. Coming home from the mall with a special selection of his favorite See's candy, planning a mystery outing, ordering a British comedy or opera DVD, all the little non-birthday, non-Christmas presents that are part of a giving partnership. I loved his surprise when I gave him a DVD of Tosca, his favorite opera, which was filmed in Verona during the very summer he saw the production. He used it in his Humanities class each semester. If you recall, Tosca's aria "Vissi d'Arte" ("I Lived for Art") was one of the symbolic songs sung at his service.

My days continue with distractions and performances (my own). I am going to use that as a title for something someday. I remember years ago asking the Santa Fe Opera Tour participants what their favorite opera was—naively thinking they were going with us for the opera. Most mumbled non-replies. I wish I could remember what Vere Wolf, our lecturer, said, but alas I have forgotten. I am thinking maybe something by Wagner or Verdi. I do remember looking sheepishly at him as I confessed my favorite was "La Boheme." I knew this wasn't the cool opera to real buffs. But the totality of it, wrapped up neatly in less than two hours and ending too soon, like life, still seems perfect to me: the recklessness and playfulness of youth; impulsive love, mercurial love, enduring love; camaraderie of true friends; art as a worthy struggle; life as a party, a challenge, and a deathbed.

Love, Ann

From: Scherr, Mary
Sent: 3/25/2005 10:56 p.m.
To: ann_carli@yahoo.com
Subject: Gibran poem

Dear Ann,

I clearly recall two routines that I followed without any conscious planning or suggestions from friends.

For nearly three months I received sympathy cards and notes every day—from friends, colleagues (his and mine), his patients, my international students. Many people were out of town over the holidays and did not know Stu had died until weeks/months later and were completely shocked since he had not been ill. Daily I sorted thru my mail and saved the personal-looking envelopes until I climbed into bed at night. I then read. The memories recounted, the gratitude expressed by patients, and the loving concern for our family soothed and comforted. I was able to fall asleep with a sense of peace that dissolved much of my sadness.

I also read a poem by Gibran that was sent to me by a friend whose young daughter had died.

Beauty of Death

Let me sleep, for my soul is intoxicated with love,
and let me rest,
  for my spirit has had its bounty of days and
  nights...

Dry your tears my friends, and raise your heads
as the flowers raise
  their crowns to greet the dawn...

I have passed a mountain peak and my soul is
soaring in the
  firmament of complete and unbounded freedom...

The songs of the waves and hymns of the streams
are scattered,
  And the voices of the throngs reduced to
  silence, and I can
  Hear naught but the music of Eternity in
  exact harmony with
  The spirit's desires.

I am cloaked in full whiteness; I am in comfort; I
am in peace...

Lament me not, but sing songs of youth and joy;
shed not tears
  Upon me, but sing of harvest and the wine
  press;

Utter no sigh of agony, but draw upon my face
with your finger
    The symbol of Love and Joy.

Disturb not the air's tranquility with chanting
and requiems,
    But let your hearts sing with me the song of
    Eternal Life;

Mourn me not with apparel of black, but dress in
color and rejoice
    With me.

Talk not of my departure with sighs in your heart;
close your eyes
    and you will see me with you forevermore...

Breathe the fragrance of my heart into space; and
reveal even to
    The sun the secret of my peace...

Go back to the joy of your dwellings and you will
find there that
    Which even Death cannot remove from you
    and me.

I read the third line of that poem every night for several weeks. I especially liked the lines because all the mystics I have ever read talk about the soul reaching complete freedom—soaring and unbounded. That's what I think of when I am at the ocean. I recall that when I said my final goodbye to Stu, I thought: I will always talk with you at the ocean. Walking along the ocean was so much a part of our life that we agreed that we wouldn't want to move away from the coast. For me, the ocean represents eternity, harmony, rhythm, and change within stability—I feel fortunate to live close enough to the ocean for daily walks. I find the serenity I need.

You, too, will find peace and serenity . . . in time.

Love, mary

From: Carli, Ann
Sent: Fri 3/27/2005 4:21 p.m.
To: MaryScherr@aol.com
Subject: Reflections

Dear Mary,

I inhaled as I read the poem by Gibran. It is
filled with peacefulness in a voice that wafts,
gently offering images that encompass the past,
the present, and the future and is filled with vivid
senses—songs and sun, flowers and mountains,
harvest and winepress, waves and streams. It is a
hymn sung by the dead to the living. It speaks to
me because it is a direct connection with nature
without an overlay of or interruption of "god."

Our recent conversations on Gibran's poem, the
ocean, rain, and my garden remind me of another
poem by Elinor Wylie. Along with the Auden poem
"Stop All the Clocks," it is my favorite poem about
death. Both Auden and Wylie have a piercing,
bittersweet aspect that speaks to me.

Farewell, Sweet Dust
Elinor Wylie

Now I have lost you, I must scatter
All of you on the air henceforth;
Not that to me it can ever matter
But it's only fair to the rest of earth.

Now especially, when it is winter
And the sun's not half so bright as he was,
Who wouldn't be glad to find a splinter
That once was you, in the frozen grass?

Snowflakes, too, will be softer feathered,
Clouds, perhaps, will be whiter plumed;
Rain, whose brilliance you caught and gathered,
Purer silver have reassumed.

Farewell, sweet dust; I was never a miser:
Once, for a minute, I made you mine:
Now you are gone, I am none the wiser
But the leaves of the willow are bright as wine.

I had planned to scatter Angelo's ashes on his birthday in March but naively was unaware that the urn is completely sealed. I called the mortuary and they will open it for a modest fee. I plan to do this. I will have to sign some legal document about the ashes but plan to circumvent the stipulations. I want to bury most of the ashes around the weeping cherries here at the house. Angelo loved his house so. Some (not many) I want to take by myself, or with the children if they want to come, to dig into a garden area at Palomar College and then in a planter at the racetrack where he worked each summer.

Earth to earth and dust to dust.

Love, Ann

From: Scherr, Mary
Sent: Tues 4/9/2005 4:29 p.m.
To: ann_carli@yahoo.com
Subject: Words

Dear Ann,

I had no idea that scattering ashes where and when you desired was so complicated. I like your plan and the reasons for multiple destinations.

The poem by Wylie beautifully expresses your thoughts these past weeks without artificially glossing over your sadness.

My gratitude to poets! Effective words are so important. They can be soothing, reassuring, rhythmical. At times the trite sayings on cards annoyed me—more accurately they irritated me. I recall one verse ending with advice not to be distressed because dying for my loved one was just like going into another room. "No, way," I protested. "If so, I could go into another room and find him." When I read that card I struggled to remember that the sender was a sincere believer sending me love and concern.

Love, mary
p.s. You're included in my gratitude. I love your poems.

From: Carli, Ann
Sent: Sat 4/12/2005 9:31 a.m.
To: MaryScherr@aol.com
Subject: Spring is Here, I Hear

Dear Mary,

Yes, words do have power far beyond Webster's Dictionary.

Here is another one of those word labyrinths. I wrote a friend that I am in some kind of limbo. As I wrote that word, I became curious about its dictionary definition. Here it is:

Limbo
1. often capitalized: an abode of souls that are according to Roman Catholic theology barred from heaven because of not having received Christian baptism

2 a: a place or state of restraint or confinement
   b: a place or state of neglect or oblivion
      <proposals kept in limbo>
   c: an intermediate or transitional place or state
   d: a state of uncertainty

All of those fit—barred from heaven; a state of restraint, neglect, oblivion, transition, uncertainty.

I feel like I drift through my days, not finding invitations inviting. My house is very neat and clean. I hate it. I realize what the missing messiness means. Various sums of money appear—"death benefit," life insurance, my reconfigured retirement. I hate the money because of what it is supposed to compensate me for.

I have been told by many others that memory is one of the functions that just doesn't work in the aftermath of great loss. There is an overall numbness and disconnection with the world. A friend wrote recently "I miss you." I responded, "I miss me too." I feel I too died.

This first week of the equinox, I think of the wonderful old Lorenz Hart song, "Spring is Here," which asks "Why doesn't my heart go dancing?" The words "No desire, no ambition leads me" describe the ennui I feel. And after the final wistful question "Why doesn't the night invite me?" the song whispers "Maybe it's because nobody loves me." Every day I see/think/feel his loss in a new way. Angelo was by my side literally and figuratively since I was 20 and he was 22. I've always counted and valued all the years we had been married but didn't factor how very young we bonded.

He was an independent and self-contained man, a paradoxical introvert with warm and expansive social skills and extraordinary character.

How fortunate I was to have had him in my life. He was the best person I ever knew.

I think of people who wish for more time, more order, more money, who don't understand that none of it is really important. Well, maybe more time...

Love, Ann

From: Scherr, Mary
Sent: 4/21/2005 10:06 p.m.
To: ann_carli@yahoo.com
Subject: Dinner Together

Dear Ann,

When I left your house last Saturday night, I recalled a friend telling me: "Your life will be different but it can be rewarding and satisfying." I left with a warm glow, a feeling of closeness and the comfort that comes from a friend who completely understands. In addition, your food and house have an exuberance that I love! Your food looked elegant, tasted superb, and the flowers were magnificent. Saturday night was a special evening and I thank you for your time and effort and willingness to share.

You wrote, "I miss me too" in your last e-mail. A succinct and oh so accurate reaction to your life now. There's a significant part of you that no longer can relate to another. Your thoughts, reactions, concerns, excitements—all those parts of your life that you shared. We both miss that part of our lives we shared with our husbands.

When Cynth left for college in the fall at the age of 17, and didn't come home until Christmas time, I recall that there was a part of me that seemed static or stagnant. Part of me was not expressed. I missed her terribly, but I also missed part of me as I realized when I read your letter. Since I was born with all the eggs that might ever become fertilized, she was a part of me when I was born!

Love, mary

From: Carli, Ann
Sent: Fri 4/22/2005 3:05 p.m.
To: MaryScherr@aol.com
Subject: Re: Dinner Together

Dear Mary,

Saturday with you and Pam was very rewarding for me. I don't cook much anymore so simple acts of gathering food and preparing it for dear friends is a pleasure.

Isn't it invigorating when three friends converse so openly? I've observed communication among a trio (or more) over the years and believe only two people are in conversation at a time. The dialogue shifts from twosome to twosome among good communicators. This happened with us. I appreciate being the "observer" because I can watch the dynamics rather than participate and being engaged has different dimensions. I'm glad you came early and stayed later so we could talk one-on-one too.

Thank you for your lovely words about the evening. I have clung to beauty since Angelo died and have heard myself saying to others "It is all I have left." I know you will understand that I do not undervalue my wonderful children and friends but they live their separate, busy lives. The

intimate synergistic life I led with Ang is gone.
My daily companion now is beauty—in a flower
arrangement or music or art. I read recently this
quote by Anne Frank: "Think of all the beauty that
is still left in and around you and be happy!" But
I am painfully aware of my lost communion in
sharing the beauty of the world. Today in the patio
I wrote this poem:

Arugula

Did you ever see an arugula blossom,
Pale yellowcream, with crimson webveins
Linking its four petalwings to tiny sixpronged crown?
You would have liked its sweetspice fragrance,
Admired its wandstalk, pungent like its leaves.
But you left before it flowered
And I wonder if you ever saw arugula in bloom.

Love, Ann

From: Scherr, Mary
Sent: Fri 4/24/2005 10:23 a.m.
To: ann_carli@yahoo.com
Subject: Meditations

Dear Ann,

Thank you, thank you for delivering an arugula in bloom along with your poem. I loved the verse—very much—poignant and oh so true. Many times I wonder if Stu saw or knew or thought something. Also the fragrance of the arugula was like a gentle memory that wafted across the table.

I'm not sure why I feel like I want to share a particular litany with you; perhaps because I found that inspirational words helped me start the day. By concentrating on a poem or litany during meditation, my mind doesn't wander everywhere quite so often. And there's an added bonus: Memorizing litanies has increased my memory. So here it is; the very first litany that I memorized:

May I wake up in the morning with the sacred word
upon my lips
May I see divinity everywhere and in everyone.
May I be inspired to choose persuasive words, loving
language,
And creative and positive thoughts to bring peace
and goodwill into the world.
May I deepen my meditation
So that I may draw upon the energy of the universe
To heal myself and the world.
May I fall asleep at night with the sacred word upon
my lips
To heal my wounds and prepare for another day of
service.

Love and Concern, mary

From: Carli, Ann
Sent: Fri 5/1/2005 8:31 p.m.
To: MaryScherr@aol.com
Subject: Re: Meditations

Dear Mary,

What would we do without language? The poems and quotations we have shared, our own stories through grief and continuance, even the struggle that people have speaking to us about death connect us through words. This line from your meditation resonates:

May I be inspired to choose persuasive words,
    loving language,
And creative and positive thoughts
To bring peace and goodwill into the world.

It reminds me of the St. Francis prayer you alluded to earlier. Although I do not pray, I love the affirmation:

Lord, make me be an instrument of Thy peace
Where there is hatred, let me sow love;
Where there is injury, pardon;
Where there is doubt, faith;
Where there is despair, hope;
Where there is darkness, light;
Where there is sadness, joy.
Grant that I may not so much seek
To be consoled as to console,
To be understood as to understand,
To be loved as to love;
For it is in giving that we receive;
It is in pardoning that we are pardoned;
And it is in dying to self that we are born to
     eternal life.

As I wrote this, Mary, it came to me that Angelo provided this instrument of peace for me, reminding me to be my better self—to forgive, to hope, to find joy. He consoled me and understood me and gave me light.

He was a great teacher.

Love, Ann

From: Carli, Ann
Sent: Wed 5/18/2005 8:05 p.m.
To: MaryScherr@aol.com
Subject: Poignant Evening

Dear Mary,

Monday evening I went to Palomar College for their literary journal awards. They dedicated the journal to Angelo with the lovely photo taken of him last November at the Veterans' Day ceremony. They gave the first place poetry award in his name. The audience was filled with his English department colleagues and the young student writers. I wept through his colleague Barbara's heartfelt remarks about him. She told a lovely story about him, beginning with, "Although Angelo loved his wife Ann, he always admired the pretty girls of spring." I knew this hearkened back to two of his favorite pieces of literature. I looked them up this evening and want to share them with you.

He thought the title of Irwin Shaw's short story "The Girls in Their Summer Dresses" was one of the best in literature. The wife in the story resents her husband appreciating other women as a sign he is not really connected to her as he claims.

This was not the case in our relationship. Of course Angelo, who appreciated beauty in all aspects of life, would appreciate a beautiful woman! I was, however, more aware of women admiring Angelo than the reverse. He would come home from grocery shopping and tell me about some woman asking him about the produce he was buying. I would laugh and say, "She was hitting on you, dear." He was so ingenuous. And that, of course, was a significant part of his charm.

Almost every year he would refer to the W. D. Snodgrass poem "April Inventory." Angelo loved the line:

> *"The sleek, expensive girls I teach,*
> *Younger and pinker every year,*
> *Bloom gradually out of reach."*

It is definitely a man's poem and, of course, especially resonant for a professor like Angelo. No doubt he had his own regrets and resignations but he lived his life with gentleness and grace. I am glad for all the young and pink students he appreciated.

Love, Ann

From: Scherr, Mary
Sent: Sun 5/22/2005 11:18 p.m.
To: ann_carli@yahoo.com
Subject: Tributes to good men

Dear Ann,

Congratulations to whoever initiated the idea of dedicating the Palomar Literary Journal, *Bravura*, to Angelo. He would have been pleased. I'm sure there were difficult moments for you, but how special to have an event that included both his colleagues and students. As you describe the evening and recall the short story and poem that were Angelo's favorites I again realized how much you and Angelo shared your mutual love of literature. In addition, you each had been both teacher and administrator in a community college. I've always thought the closest marriages were those in which both husband and wife were in the same field. You were blessed.

A few months after Stu died, the Pacific Coast Band in which he had played clarinet for many years, dedicated the Brahms Requiem to Stu during their spring concert. They also invited Andrew, my son-in-law, to sing the baritone solo. I opened the concert program, saw Stu's picture and a tribute to him, and cried silently during the rest of the concert. How difficult, yet I was very appreciative of the wonderful tribute from his musician friends. They are special people.

We're fortunate that thoughtful friends arranged meaningful tributes to our husbands.

Love, mary

From: Carli, Ann
Sent: Mon 5/23/2005 5:29 p.m.
To: MaryScherr@aol.com
Subject: Re: Tributes to good men

Dear Mary,

I too am impressed that both our husbands were honored in memoriam by friends who shared their love of art. I heard Stu play in the college orchestra many times and was so impressed with his making time in his busy medical life to play in two musical groups. Conversations drift back to me, Mary. I remember his being critical of the local classical radio station because "they played the same pieces over and over." He would have approved of the Brahms Requiem.

Yes, Angelo's and my careers were very similar. At one time we were both Deans of Community Education at our respective colleges! We collaborated on and co-sponsored community events. I often thought we were the only administrators who didn't feel competitive with each other's nearby college.

Our backgrounds as English majors were another bond. We read very different books for recreation but would share beautifully written passages.

Ah, books, I sit here looking at 3,000 of his books in what was his "study"—a euphemism at best—not wanting to think what I will do with the other 7,000, he collected and stored in the garage plus a storage unit.

Philip is coming out in July to help with the "divestiture." Like Scarlett O'Hara, I will think about that tomorrow!

Love, Ann

Summer

From: Scherr, Mary
Sent: Thurs 6/2/2005 8:18 a.m.
To: ann_carli@yahoo.com
Subject: First summer

Dear Ann,

Summer is almost here with a different set of memories. After my five years or even your five months the majority of friends think we have gone beyond grief, a word I never used. I think I have already said that grief sounds like an acute state that is temporary but I was aware of pervasive sadness I expected to last at least intermittently all the rest of my life.

I often taught international students in the summer and loved inviting them for brunch on Saturday as Stu thoroughly enjoyed hosting and visiting. Good memories of long conversations on the deck that lasted most of the afternoon. Pat, who was one of the First Nation women from Canada, explained some of the Cree symbolism to me. That is why I have positive connotations with mountains and why I often wear a mountain charm, along with other favorite charms, on a long gold chain. It does remind me that I have strength.

Did Angelo teach in the summer? Was your schedule substantially different? Stu's schedule remained the same 12 months of the year! It takes mental effort to be grateful, instead of merely nostalgic, for the summer experiences we shared. I have slowly become more successful but the first summer is not easy.

Thinking of you and sending love, mary

From: Carli, Ann
Sent: Tues 6/3/2005 3:22 p.m.
To: MaryScherr@aol.com
Subject: Summer

Dear Mary,

I dread summer. The heat, the fewer demands when I worked as an academic, the slower pace have always enervated me. Angelo spent his summers working at the racetrack and I felt like I was always waiting—for him to come home at 7 p.m., waiting for Tuesdays, his only day off, waiting for the track season to end and our life to return to normal. He loved the milieu, the people, watching the beautiful horses run all day. He would come home with wonderful stories about the events of the day; I told him he should write about them but he never did.

I've been thinking about those sudden flashes of this non-reality of Angelo being gone. Every day there is something. I don't think I will ever reconcile myself that his vital being has left the earth, has left me.

When I remarked to a friend recently about the small jolts throughout the day, saying, "Every day …" my friend sympathetically responded, "Every moment…" but I quietly replied "No, not every moment. Sometimes I am busy."

This is my dark poem about this:

Trigger

The angled sun and a certain breeze
Joggles the visor, topples the ease.
Never the date, nor your name aloud,
Not the daily photo, nor the nightly shroud.
But a waft of light and a beam of draft,
A current's flurry and a solar shaft,
A sweep of wind, a stroke of the sun,
Deafens and blinds like the shot of a gun.

Love, Ann

From: Scherr, Mary
Sent: 7/8/2005 3:30 p.m.
To: ann_carli@yahoo.com
Subject: Re: Summer

Dear Ann,

I'm not only home, I'm unpacked and mostly caught up with mail. Our stay in Ireland was wonderful. Everyone got along fine. No minor accomplishment considering nine independent, very different personalities. Janet and Cynthia each came with their families for one week and overlapped in the middle. The tiny village of Clohaun was delightful.

Today I was thinking of you and recalling how I spent my first summer alone.

I remember that I went to Oregon the end of June and stayed through July 4th. I was glad that I had a friend my age in Ashland. I enjoyed spending some time with her as I sometimes felt like an "extra" even though Cynthia's family is warm and loving and made me feel very welcome. Feeling single is a strange emotion after 40 years of marriage. A single friend told me: "People like even numbers so pairs are preferred!"

Later that summer I attended my first, weeklong silent retreat. After Stu died, I began meditating in earnest and was pleased to discover I entered a serene state, but I lacked the discipline to be consistent on a daily basis. I had read several books by Thich Nhat Hahn, so when I learned he was leading a retreat, I registered at UCSD. Bobbie, a very close friend, offered to attend with me. She and her husband live close to campus and invited me to be their houseguest. The guest room was filled with flowers and on the bed were two tiny bears announcing, "Best friends are forever!" The warmth of their hospitality was very comforting and I loved Bobbie's companionship during the week.

I attended a "grief" discussion group. On the first afternoon, each person briefly told his/her story. By the time it became my turn, I felt I had little cause for major distress. I did not have small children to raise alone nor did I need to find a way to support myself for the first time. Also, I had strong support from daughters, friends, and colleagues at work.

Although I have facilitated a weekend retreat for women each spring for the last nine years, I only began to meditate daily after Stu died. More recently a small group of us have been meditating together once a month. I had no idea how deep communication can be without words. What began as the result of a drastic change in my life has now become a spiritual practice that is enriching my life.

Love, mary

From: Carli, Ann
Sent: Sat 7/9/2005 5:30 p.m.
To: MaryScherr@aol.com
Subject: Summer Retreat

Dear Mary,

I'm so glad for your wonderful family vacation
in Ireland. What a clever idea of each family
having time alone with time in-between together. It
obviously worked as everyone got along well.

I have found that my adult children can fall into
old patterns of their childhood: impatience, overly
sensitive feelings, opinion rivalry. They care deeply
for each other but are such different temperaments.
I could deal with these regressions better with
Angelo by my side when we could bolster each
other through them.

That shared reality is something I miss
terribly—understanding our kids' peccadilloes,
appreciating a great joke, enjoying good movies
and good television, criticizing bad movies and
bad television, discerning a fine from a not-so-fine
operatic voice, seeing through political obfuscation
and religious hypocrisy, pondering and processing
philosophical questions, relishing good pasta.
I keep thinking, "Angelo would like this" or
"Angelo would hate this." Every day there is

something new to miss so I started a list I've titled, "All the things…"

While your family was enjoying the Irish countryside, we were clearing the double storage unit Angelo had rented for his overflow "collectibles." These included turntables, bicycles, sports equipment, tools, records, framed art, furniture, neon signs, old radios, and about 3,000 books. I am not exaggerating, Mary. I had no idea what he had stored there and it was a shock. We rented a van and moved it all home, stuffing it into the already packed garage. Philip was here from Rochester to help and we had a driveway sale. We got rid of everything, saving the books for another sale because there are another 7,000, including the boxes he had stored in our garage and house.

I could have used your meditation! I just kept reminding myself that this was Angelo's only "vice" and he spent many happy hours of his life finding "bargains." Did I ever tell you that he actually did have two very important finds? He found first editions of Malthus' *An Essay on the Principle of Population* and Adam Smith's *An Inquiry into the Nature and Causes of the Wealth of Nations*. He auctioned them through Sotheby's in New York and the proceeds paid for a good deal of the kids' education. I vowed then I would never again complain about his book hunts or the garage we could not park in. And I never did.

Love, Ann

From: Scherr, Mary
Sent: 7/21/2005 10:10 p.m.
To: ann_carli@yahoo.com
Subject: Psychological slump

Dear Ann,

    We share an interest in language—responding to the power of words and realizing the solace that comes from hearing a phrase that resonates closely with our feelings as opposed to worn out expressions.

    I have been in a psychological slump for the last four days. Not typical for me at all. I have not accomplished anything. I've been daydreaming and taking naps. Also remembering events of long ago. I recalled that when I conducted interviews for my dissertation, I asked women what "maturity" meant to them. One woman explained: "I want to continually strive to reach my potential. I want to feel that I am a better teacher every year . . . and I hope to help my parents conclude their lives in satisfying ways." My own parents were in their middle eighties at the time. I had thought mostly in terms of physically helping them, writing checks, and buying groceries. I was impressed with my interviewee's commitment to her elderly parents in a far more meaningful way than mine.

I think that memory was auspicious. I plan to conclude life in a satisfying way by engaging in meaningful projects. Bishop Spong, one of my favorite writers, was asked after one of his lectures, "What is the main purpose in life?" To which he answered, "Become all that you can become; love unconditionally; and live fully."

When I was in my twenties, I hoped to "find someone." I hoped to marry and have children. My idea of future happiness was linked to a husband. After the good fortune of having a husband and children—and now being alone after 40 years, I realize my happiness cannot be linked to a husband, partner, or mate. My happiness must be found within me. Which, of course, all the spiritual advisors and mystics have said for hundreds of years. A friend gave me a web site reference to "retreat gardens." I'd like to improve my garden, create a meditation walk, and continue to offer my house for meditation groups and small community meetings.

Also, this week I realized that the decision to retire triggered feelings of aloneness—no structured daily interaction with colleagues as well as a loss of status and title. I need to turn that deficit into a bonus and think of the options I will have because I am not committed to full time work… So… I think the slump caused some repressed feelings to surface so that I can deal with them. Therefore, I accomplished a lot by not accomplishing anything physically tangible. Also, I investigated the possibility of a phased retirement and concluded that a half time contract would be an excellent way to transition into full time retirement. I am fortunate that that is an option at USD.

I had a good time in the Northwest, saw Janet's new house, and am more impressed with Seattle each time I visit. Seeing Natalie is always inspiring! Creative and fun and exuberant. When do you go to New York?

Take care and love, mary

From: Carli, Ann
Sent: Fri 7/22/2005 2:12 p.m.
To: MaryScherr@aol.com
Subject: Re: Psychological slump

Dear Mary,

This must be our mutual season of discontent because this past week has been one of those descents to the absolute bottom for me. I can never anticipate what will bring this on, but in retrospect two experiences should have been predictors. One was my second foray in doing 2004 taxes, for which I had an extension. I worked furtively to prepare for what I thought would be Meeting #2 with the CPA. Angelo always gathered this information so this was a huge job for me, especially since 2004 was a complicated year. As it turned out, I actually completed the job and did not have to go back to the CPA for Meeting #3.

The second experience was trying to find the receipt for the malfunctioning television Angelo had purchased last September. I spent one entire day going through files, calling the electronics store, getting shuffled from recorded number to recorded number. There was a happy ending to that story too. I finally found the bill and now have an appointment for the repair. I can tell you, though, both these experiences had me in tears, bringing up so many logistics of life that I must now figure out on my own.

Every day I stumble and fall into another hollow of my cave, this dark place where Angelo is so painfully absent.

Today I was explaining to a friend that Angelo handled almost all of the business of life because he was retired and I was still working. When I added, "Now I have to figure out and do all of what he did plus continue the parts of life I handled," she said quietly, "And you are doing what he didn't do too." Whoosh. Clearing his double storage unit, filled to the gunnels with his stuff; strategizing what to do with the triple car garage filled with his books plus the bookcases in the house, totaling 10,000 volumes; initiating two necessary and big house repair projects. These were his goals and objectives, but he ran out of time.

Your reflections on maturity resonate with me, especially in regards to our generation's script that husband/partner = happiness. In my Women's Studies classes I used to teach the pitfall of women tying one's status and identity to a spouse—but only in terms of divorce. I used the example of Mrs. XYZ being replaced by a new Mrs. XYZ. However, I never thought of the changes in status and identity in terms of the death of a spouse.

Happiness seems so elusive to me now because Angelo is gone. Here I am this "liberated" woman feeling like I have lost so much of myself—not for losing a husband per se but losing the mirror who knew me, loved me with all my faults, taught and inspired me to my better self.

When we would fight, which was rarely, I always felt so alone and would actually say to Angelo what you have written: "Ultimately each of us is alone." I've known this since I was a very young child because I really wasn't parented and was left alone most of the time. My father was an alcoholic and my mother worked long hours to support the family. But even with this philosophical conviction of aloneness, I was and am unprepared for being alone without him. I always described our marriage relationship as interdependent, rather than independent or dependent. Doesn't that sound "mature"? Yet the definition of interdependent is "mutually dependent" and dependent means "determined or conditioned by another" and "relying on another for support." So maybe interdependence wasn't so wise? But to hold his warm hand, if only briefly, in this cold universe, I would still choose it.

I'm glad your trip to Seattle held so many good experiences for you.

My New York trip is scheduled for the last week in September (September 30–October 6) and is the first stirring of anticipation I have felt in a year.

Thank you for the opportunity for these reflections, Mary.

Love, Ann

From: Scherr, Mary
Sent: 8/11/2005 9:51 p.m.
To: ann_carli@yahoo.com
Subject: Happiness

Dear Ann,

Recognizing psychological slumps and considering their triggers often causes us to think more carefully about personal happiness, don't you think?

I recall writing you that during the first winter of feeling so much alone I invited a woman over for dinner whose husband had died about nine months earlier. Since then I have resolved to reach out to others instead of focusing on my own aloneness. A couple of years ago, as I approached Mother's Day, I thought of how much I'd like to be with my daughters, but they do not live nearby. So I mentally ran through a list of my single women friends who do not have local children and I invited two for lunch on Mother's Day. I used best dishes, arranged lovely flowers, prepared a special entrée, and thoroughly enjoyed the preparation. Both of the women were appreciative.

As I write these anecdotes, I realize there's a basic truth in them, but the greatest source of happiness for me comes from a more sustained commitment. I strongly agree with the last two lines of "To Be of Use" by Marge Piercy.

To Be of Use
Marge Piercy

The people I love the best
jump into work head first
without dallying in the shallows
and swim off with sure strokes almost out of sight.
They seem to become natives of that element,
the black sleek heads of seals
bouncing like half-submerged balls.

I love people who harness themselves, an ox to a
*   heavy cart,*
who pull like water buffalo, with massive patience,
who strain in the mud and the muck to move things
*   forward,*
who do what has to be done, again and again.

I want to be with people who submerge
in the task, who go into the fields to harvest
and work in a row and pass the bags along,
who stand in the line and haul in their places,
who are not parlor generals and field deserters
but move in a common rhythm
when the food must come in or the fire be put out.

The work of the world is common as mud.
Botched, it smears the hands, crumbles to dust.

But the thing worth doing well done
has a shape that satisfies, clean and evident.
Greek amphoras for wine or oil,
Hopi vases that held corn, are put in museums
but you know they were made to be used.
The pitcher cries for water to carry
and a person for work that is real.

Love, mary

From: Carli, Ann
Sent: Thurs 8/12/2005 4:30 p.m.
To: MaryScherr@aol.com
Subject: Re: Happiness

Dear Mary,

What a wonderful poem! Each time I read
it I find something new—and something old. It
brought to mind one of the "scripts" from my
father, "If you are going to do something, do it
well." It has always felt like a challenge rather than
a criticism to me but I often feel like I fall short of
the mark. Work and love—isn't that what Freud
said was the source of happiness?

I like discussing happiness with you and want
to continue this as we go along. I listened recently
to a lecture on CD from "The Great Courses
series." The professor, Daniel Robinson from
Oxford, outlined various philosophical theories
of the good life, i.e., happiness. His conclusion,
synthesized from various philosophies, was
that the good life has four components: 1) a
contemplative life 2) an active life 3) a "somewhat
fatalistic view of life" (accepting the slings and
arrows of outrageous fortune) and 4) a life of
service (living with the best interests of others
in mind). This is not a good summary but his

lecture was so effective I am going to buy the course on CD.

The third fatalistic component surprised me in this context although it is a view I have held all my life. Even with this enormous loss, I realize it is the randomness of life that a truly good man would die young. I've never been one to even consider the question "Why?"

However, I can't help but think there should be a fifth component for a good life, one of connectedness—not necessarily marriage but a deep connection with another. Your Bishop Spong's "love unconditionally" would encapsulate this for me and Marge Piercy's people who "move in common rhythm."

Coming back to maturity, do you think happiness could be maturity and vice versa?

There is so much in your letter that I want to discuss, especially your reflections about retirement and the anticipated changes in your life structure, role, title, and status. That's such a big and important topic and certainly tied to our pondering happiness. I will return to it later with the hope we can explore it together.

Love, Ann

"Three grand essentials to happiness in this life are something to do, something to love, and something to hope for."
Joseph Addison

From: Scherr, Mary
Sent: 8/21/2005 8:41 p.m.
To: ann_carli@yahoo.com
Subject: fairy gardens

Dear Ann,

I worked in the yard all morning and saw that the fairy gardens were still designated by the initials of each of my three grandchildren. Natalie was here most recently and so her "N" is in the best shape.

When Natalie was almost three, I introduced her to the idea of a fairy garden. She placed her initial in stones at the entrance to an area enclosed by bushes and hidden from the house. The initial indicated to the fairy that she was in residence!

Early the next morning we hurried down to the garden to see what the fairy left. She found three tiny presents in the branches! A special stone, a sand dollar, and a tiny pinecone. The fairy nearly always brought natural objects from land or sea.

Every morning she was here, we ran down to the garden as soon as it was light enough to see. Once at Easter time all three of my grandchildren were here and I scrambled to find nine little presents to hide each night. Derek and Kathryn no longer believe in garden fairies, but they pretend. I wrote the following directions for Derek and Kathryn when they were four and six.

Down at the bottom of the stairs you'll see
An old and sprawling lemon tree,
Turn to your left, go around the curve
Three stair steps are right ahead
Leading along a flowerbed.

Two more steps and stop right there
Where the path goes left and also right
The plant with flowers, oh, so blue
Rosemary, rosemary that is true.

Take three giant steps straight ahead
See the entrance to Kate's little hideaway.
If Derek turns and goes to his left
Nine giant steps and he will be
Right beside a letter "D"

Grandmothers have a wonderful excuse to become engaged with magic, fairies, and secret gardens. A grandchild lets the child within us spring forth! I'm so glad you are expecting a grandson this fall.

Love, mary

From: Carli, Ann
Sent: Mon 8/22/2005 1:16 p.m.
To: MaryScherr@aol.com
Subject: Re: fairy gardens

Dear Mary,

Our grandchildren remind us that the world can be a magical place. What enchantment you provide for Natalie, Kate, and Derek! They will remember the fairy gardens all their lives and tell their grandchildren about their grandmother's special connection to the fairy world.

Love, Ann

Autumn

From: Scherr, Mary
Sent: Mon 9/12/2005 10:52 p.m.
To: ann_carli@yahoo.com
Subject: retirement

Dear Ann,

As I mentioned several e-mails ago, I was surprised to experience mild depression this summer. I finally realized that it was partially related to my retirement plans. But after going back to work and sitting thru a "retreat day" with the entire school, I smiled to myself when I realized I would not need to attend meetings which so rarely are energizing much longer. Completely programmed large groups with no opportunity to share ideas with a few department colleagues are frustrating. Next year I begin "phased retirement" and teach only in the spring.

I do, however, always get excited about the start of a new year. September is the beginning of a new year for me; not January! I have taught so long that psychologically I follow the rhythm of an academic calendar.

I love working with graduate students and feel very fortunate to have been a part of the leadership studies programs for 17 years. I have taught the classes I wanted, read the books and articles I would have read whether or not I was teaching, and learned a great deal from my experienced, adult students. Also, I value the relationships with both students and faculty.

As I left for San Diego yesterday morning, I suddenly recalled my mother telling me that during the first years of her marriage, she always had tears in her eyes when children walked by her house in September with school books under their arms. She taught in the days when married women were not allowed to teach.

And I also recalled that during the depression she couldn't get a job because she had only three years of college. She strongly encouraged me to continue in college until I earned a master's degree because she reasoned that a Master's in my generation was probably the equivalent to a Bachelor's degree in her time. When I was 49 I told her I was going back to school to earn a doctoral degree. She grinned widely and announced: "That's what I would do!" I was extremely fortunate to have her enthusiastic support as well as Stu's support and encouragement throughout my doctoral program.

Love, mary

From: Carli, Ann
Sent: Tues 9/13/2005 4:15 p.m.
To: MaryScherr@aol.com
Subject: September Reflections

Dear Mary,

Like you, September, rather than January, has always seemed like the "New Year." Every fall semester for the twenty-seven years of my college career I would buy something new to wear for the first day of "school." It always brought back that excitement of childhood.

I would also buy Angelo a new tie. He was probably the only guy in the English department that wore a tie and had an impressive collection, thanks to me. He enjoyed the attention he would get from students, especially with some of my more creative choices. He had one black and white with question marks all over it and a Christmas tie with Santas and a tiny music box that played jingle bells.

His ties were a trademark and a hallmark, I think, as he was a very traditional teacher. Unlike his colleagues who used their first names with students, Angelo insisted on being called Mr. Carli and always addressed his students as Mr. or Ms. He didn't do this lightly; he was trying to instill a sense of responsibility as well as grammar. I described him as an Old Tyme Teacher.

As could be expected, students were divided in their response to his formality. He was a dedicated and fine teacher but was clear that was his role. The later generation of students who were searching for therapy or self-esteem did not find it in his classroom.

He was a great storyteller in the classroom and out. One of my favorites captured the dilemma of Generation X students and the old-fashioned teacher. It involved a student who would arrive with a huge cup of coffee every class. Mid-way through Angelo's lecture the student would inevitably get up from his seat and leave the classroom, shortly to return. As a teacher yourself, you can imagine how distracting these interruptions were. Finally, Ang asked the student to stay a few minutes after class and addressed the problem. The fellow explained he had to get up because he needed to go to the bathroom. Angelo waited a few seconds and then said, "Well, it seems to me you have three options. One, go to the bathroom before class. Two, don't drink coffee during the class. And three, hold it like a big person." I thought this was hilarious, but evidently the student didn't. He dropped the class.

I have to say, however, that Angelo was not impervious to losing students but those that stayed respected him and learned English.

This was a fun story to tell, Mary, evoking other wonderful anecdotes and even a smile.

Love, Ann

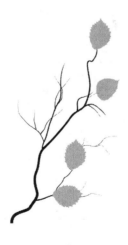

From: Scherr, Mary
Sent: Mon 9/19/2005 8:11 p.m.
To: ann_carli@yahoo.com
Subject: Fall semester

Dear Ann,

I didn't know that side of Angelo at all. I knew
he was a great teacher but didn't know he took a
more traditional role than most community college
professors. I loved the anecdote about the bathroom.
Seems to me he pointed out reasonable options!

What is your schedule this fall at MiraCosta College?
Whenever I think about MiraCosta, I recall one of the
community courses I taught in the early seventies.

I arrived at the community room in the public
library to teach a course entitled: "Changing
Patterns in Women's Lives." I began writing an
agenda on the board while a representative from
the college enrolled the women for the class. After
only a few minutes, I heard shuffling noises behind
me. I turned around to see three women hurriedly
gathering up cloth bags and purses. "This is not
what we thought at all," one woman blurted out.
"We thought you would teach us how to change our
sewing patterns."

The president of the college told me several years
later that this was his favorite anecdote to illustrate

that North San Diego County was not in the forefront of the women's movement.

Are you working three days a week? I'll be interested in hearing how it goes.

Love, mary

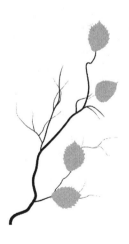

From: Carli, Ann
Sent: Mon 9/19/2005 11:09 p.m.
To: MaryScherr@aol.com
Subject: Re: Fall semester

Dear Mary,

In answer to your question about my temporary assignment at the college, this is my third week and I am counting the weeks until December 16! When I retired after twenty-seven years I left on a high, but was very ready to leave.

Two months after I retired Angelo was diagnosed with cancer. He had been retired seven years and we looked forward to travel and the simple pleasures of life together. But we had only five short months.

In terms of work, I am working half time, generally going in for three part days. I am able to focus on a direct issue, like evaluating an instructor and writing the report, or analyzing alternate solutions to a problem presented to me. But the meetings driven by information bytes and circuitous discussions are coma producing. Meetings were always an endurance trial for me but they are more so now. I have always loved projects, the creative thinking, the organization, the teamwork and then the product, but most meetings do not produce even an idea.

I am in a very knotted sense of being. Nothing matters, yet I want to have predictability in what doesn't matter! That probably doesn't make sense to anyone but me. It is akin to my being insistent on being congruent as with the grief question. This is a trait I have always had but now is beyond deadly earnest, beyond deadly honest. What could be beyond deadly? Dead?

I want to continue talking about your transition in working this year. Your response to the retreat is very interesting to me. It's good you can observe objectively and, at the same time, look forward to the year. I think you would find it useful to keep a journal of this last year at the university.

Ecclesiastes had it right: to everything there is a season.

Love, Ann

From: Scherr, Mary
Sent: Mon 9/26/2005 9:48 p.m.
To: ann_carli@yahoo.com
Subject: Sensuality and Sexuality

Dear Ann,

After houseguests and starting a new semester, I'm finally ready to get back to the rhythm of writing e-mails to you. I find these exchanges rewarding.

After five years, the desire for intimacy still sweeps over me like a wave at unpredictable times: Seeing a couple my age holding hands at the beach; watching an animated conversation between a couple at dinner; seeing a man and woman whisper and then break into hearty laughter. Holding hands, close hugs, and random touching that happens when you live together are important forms of intimacy that I miss.

After Stu died I often in the evening wrapped myself in a soft throw that Annie had given me. And in the mornings I often wore Stu's cuddly navy bathrobe. Years ago an older friend whose husband had died told me that soft fabrics that caressed the skin were comforting. After three months, I decided the robe made me sad and I sent it off to the DAV telling myself that some man might need a good robe.

Have we talked about sex? Sexual desire sure doesn't cease even when a husband is deceased.

Did I ever tell you the advice I received at the reception following Stu's memorial service? As you'll recall, nearly 200 people came to the house. At one point when the living room was crowded, I stepped outside to talk to the people on the deck. One of the women whose husband had died a couple of years before, told me without any anticipatory prelude: "You need to buy a good vibrator right away." I have no idea what I replied, but I was keenly aware that sex was not on my mind.

Now, thinking back over that first year, I wonder whether or not buying a vibrator might have been a good idea. I never did so I'll never know.

I hope all is going well and your time with Philip and family is good—very good.

Love, mary

From: Carli, Ann
Sent: Tues 9/27/2005 9:22 p.m.
To: MaryScherr@aol.com
Subject: Re: Sensuality and Sexuality

Dear Mary,

So many interesting parts of your letter. Do
you know I wear Angelo's bathrobe! I bought
this cashmere robe for him the November before
he died and gave it to him as an early Christmas
present. He had lost weight and felt cold most of
the time. He only got to wear it three months.

Libido is such a mystery. I have known friends
who quickly sought a new partner after the death
of their spouse. I think this need had many facets,
including validation, discomfort in going places
alone, as well as sexual desire. Although I do
miss Angelo's physical love, it is not high on my
list of what I long for. What I intensely miss is the
complete understanding we shared, the acceptance
and patience of each other's faults, our similar
taste and perspective of the world, our mutual
values and priorities in life. We both groaned over
banal writing or lyrics, turned the channel off
politicians' non-answers, knew when to leave a bad
movie, simultaneously winced when a singer was
off-key. Although he was the conservative parent
and I the liberal, we presented a unified front to

our children, who were our shared mission in life, through struggles and joys. Although he was the introvert and I the extrovert, we had a system where he didn't "have to" go to social events, but would if it really was important to me. And I would stoically wait as he scoured thrift shops and used bookstores. He did this the year we drove across the country and we ended up with a trunk and back seat full of books. I still get pangs when I see his local haunts—the Salvation Army, Disabled Veterans, Goodwill.

Getting back to sex, I did laugh with some astonishment at the woman's advice at Stu's memorial—of all places! One of these days you and I should have a couple of drinks and visit a sex shop. Who knows what we might learn.

For now, I am just grateful for the fulfilling sex life I had and in some ways am grateful for my quiet libido.

Love, Ann

From: Scherr, Mary
Sent: Thurs 10/6/2005 11:34 p.m.
To: ann_carli@yahoo.com
Subject: Are you home?

Dear Ann,

"Would you like to drink wine?" I had asked nearly a month ago. Your spontaneous acceptance evolved into a light supper and meaningful conversation vanished all my thoughts about a meaningless day. I was so pleased you were available and as always, I loved our conversation.

Now I have lost track of your schedule. Are you home? I think you may actually be out of town and in New York at this time.

Whenever I think of my early marriage days in New York, I recall a New Yorker cartoon that was published during our first summer in Syracuse.

The cartoon showed a woman running along the beach and calling out, "Help, help, my son the doctor is drowning." I laughed out loud and during the next year I gradually realized that my new husband had indeed grown up in a family that valued, maybe over-valued the importance of becoming a doctor.

The cartoon also helped me understand the anxiety my mother-in-law faced while Stu was applying for medical school. He learned he was accepted to his top two choices, Northwestern and Cornell. He also had taken a New York State exam for a medical scholarship.

Knowing that all applicants were anxious to learn if they had been admitted to a medical school, Stu felt he should make his decision as early as possible and release one spot. He was sure he did not do well enough on the exam to merit a scholarship for a New York medical school. His parents wanted him to wait for the results, but Stu accepted Northwestern and so declined acceptance at Cornell. Two days later he learned he had earned a scholarship for a medical school in New York.

Fortunately, he was able to reverse his decision and attend Cornell with the benefit of a scholarship. His parents had been completely agitated by his early decision and felt it indicated he did not look out for his own interests. Over the years I learned that his strong sense of what he considered fair guided his actions without equivocation.

I hope you are having a great vacation. Write or phone when you return.

Love, mary

From: Carli, Ann
Sent: Fri 10/7/2005 8:07 p.m.
To: MaryScherr@aol.com
Subject: Home!

Dear Mary,

I just returned from my first vacation without Angelo, to New York. I had known for months that this was where I wanted to go. It was only in retrospect that I understand why. As my friend Julie and I drove in to the city from JFK, I saw so many avenues I had traveled with Angelo. He was born and raised in Brooklyn. He introduced me to his parents there before we were married and we lived there the summer before Angelo began teaching. I realized this was why I had wanted to go there, of all places, on this my first venture. It was his city.

How he would have loved the art, at the Frick and MOMA, "Manon" at the Met, the zaniness of "Spamalot," the Immigrant Museum in Greenwich Village, the wonderful food, the winding walks through Central Park, jazz at the Blue Note.

He took me to meet his parents in January of 1960 and showed me the city. We had a date to go with friends to Basin Street East to hear Peggy Lee sing but there was such a blizzard they canceled. We decided to brave the storm and went by subway from Brooklyn. It was one of the most memorable and romantic nights in my life. The birthday before he became ill I found a CD of Lee's live performance during that gig and wrote this poem for him:

Snow Queen

The worst snowstorm in twenty years
falls my first trip to New York City.
Unlike the glass-domed souvenirs,
flurrying sugary crystals
onto Empire State and Chrysler pinnacles,
this snow sheets down plaster walls to ghost through.
Only lunatics and tourists venture out,
but Peggy is singing in Manhattan
and we are bound to go.
I wear velvet and fake fur,
he borrows his father's overcoat,
and we take the subway
from Brooklyn to 52nd Street.
The smoke-hazed nightclub
holds tables for three hundred
and every seat is prime.
Amber brandy splashed with Crème de Menthe
seems warming on this wintry night.
Pacing the three-drink minimum would be wise.
The room darkens and holds its breath
as the overture rises with spotlight moon
on her, turning slowly in an ivory gown.
She begins the set without a word,
Day In, Day Out, slaloming
the lyrics, the drums, the bass.
After the first number,

she greets the audience in her cinnamon voice,
seductive lips betraying her shy smile,
curled slightly to the left.
Her hair, upswept in drifts of platinum,
reverberates the light,
like sequins on her gown.
From Fever to Is That All There Is,
two hours of song.
She thanks the audience
for coming out on such a night
and buys the house a drink,
my fourth Stinger of the evening—
a flurry of another kind.
She sings another hour:
My Romance, I Love Being Here With You.
I hold the hand of the man I would marry,
the man who would carry me
two blocks in the snow that white night.

How glad I am that I gave him that poem.

I can't say I behaved "royally" that night.
After all those stingers I was in pretty bad shape.
Moreover, I had neglected to go the restroom before
leaving the nightclub. As we waited for the 3 a.m.
subway, I said to Angelo "I have to pee." And then I
did. Right there on the platform of the C train!

When I think back to that experience, I wonder
that Angelo didn't reconsider marrying such a
foolish girl.

Love, Ann

From: Scherr, Mary
Sent: Mon 10/10/2005 2:35 p.m.
To: ann_carli@yahoo.com
Subject: Shadows

Dear Ann,

Your hilarious narrative contrasted with your remarkably detailed poem clearly shows the significance of that night. How fortunate that you wrote it for him.

I am so glad you had a wonderful New York trip. Interesting that we both associate New York City with our husbands. Stu's city, I would often think. He grew up in New Rochelle but went to Cornell Medical School in The City.

We spent a brief honeymoon in New York before Stu started his residency in Syracuse. I wanted to avoid New York subways no matter how inconvenient. "If there was an emergency people would come floating up like sardines," I told him. He laughed at the absurd image and reported the number of people who travel the subways without incident. The very next day, headlines reported a flood in a subway and the need to evacuate.

Reading your e-mail is always stimulating. Have a good weekend,

Love, mary

From: Carli, Ann
Sent: Sat 10/15/2005 7:35 p.m.
To: MaryScherr@aol.com
Subject: Re: Shadows

Dear Mary,

The thought struck me recently that I had three more years with Angelo than you had with Stu. Because you and your children are/were slightly older, I thought you had more time together. You deserved more time. And so did we. But looking at the disasters in the world, I know there is no "deserving." There is only, as a friend wrote to me in condolence, "wretched fate." The injustice didn't come as a surprise to me. I've never asked why. How could I in light of history's thousands of years of tragic losses? Sometimes when I wake in the middle of the night I mentally travel the globe, continent by continent, reminding myself of the great suffering in Africa, Asia, the Middle East, the Balkans, South America, parts of Europe and this country. I say a little prayer, in my agnostic sort of way, which gets me through my shadowy night.

Love, Ann

From: Scherr, Mary
Sent: Sat 11/2/2005 5:44 p.m.
To: ann_carli@yahoo.com
Subject: Another Perspective

Dear Ann,

Oh no, I must protest, my friend. I think there is much more than "wretched fate." I believe grief or illness or coming to terms with aging can lead us down to our inner core or spirit where truth is embedded—where we encounter our true Self by becoming quiet enough to hear an inner voice.

I meet two of the conditions for journeying downward because I've experienced grief and at age 75 I am forced to recognize my own aging. Both can contribute to wisdom. I've always resisted the cliché "no pain, no gain," but must acknowledge now that a degree of darkness is necessary for spiritual growth. Theodore Roethke wrote: "In a dark time, the eye begins to see." And one of the word roots for wisdom is veda which means to see, to know.

Silence, solitude, and meditation help me hear my inner voice, and I have found gradually lets me see my shadow side. Not comfortable insights but important ones. I reacted so strongly to that last line of yours about "wretched fate," that I needed to respond, sharing more than preaching, I hope.

Love, mary

From: Carli, Ann
Sent: Tues 11/8/2005 6:02 p.m.
To: MaryScherr@aol.com
Subject: Another Season…

Dear Mary,

As the days shorten, I think back to last
year and the weekly trips to UCLA for Angelo's
chemotherapy. In spite of knowing his cancer was
called "the silent killer" we held onto hope. Those
drives to Los Angeles on Sunday afternoons and
back home Monday late mornings in the soft light
of autumn were special times for us to talk.

On Veterans Day, Palomar College, where
Angelo worked for 34 years, honored him for
his work in initiating and coordinating veterans
programs in the 70s. He spoke briefly and I was
surprised to hear him say in his thirty-year career
as a teacher and administrator, he was most proud
of his work for veterans. The last photograph I have
of him was taken at that ceremony.

The liquid amber trees are turning and I pulled
out a poem I wrote twenty years ago for a friend
whose husband had died. Now it is also a poem
for me.

Leave Taking

I think of you when November
Is jacketed in liquid amber patchwork,
A variegated time
With fall and winter zigzagging
Like the fringed edge of sleep.

I want to sew the leaves on trees,
Cajole the jays to stay,
And hypnotize the sun
At fifty-seven degrees.

But comes the shedding time,
Turning and leaving,
And turning
But leaving at the eleventh hour.

I will gather only three:
One tinged green with memories of spring,
A golden summer hand,
One fine fall fire.
The rest I leave to comfort the cold world.

Love, Ann

From: Scherr, Mary
Sent: Sat 11/19/2005 9:31 p.m.
To: ann_carli@yahoo.com
Subject: grandchildren

Dear Ann,

I always respond to your poems. I hope you'll publish them.

I've been thinking how fortunate you are to be expecting a grandson—the anticipation of a grandchild a few months after our husbands died is another one of the experiences we share—this time a happy one.

When my grandchildren were born, I recall that the experience triggered memories of the stories I had heard of my own birth and of my father's reaction to the birth of his children. I wrote the following poem on my flight home after visiting my new grandson in Alexandria.

Poem for a newborn

In the quiet of night
Toward the softness of dawn
A special time… to hold, to see, to be
With a new born child.
A little hand the length of my thumb
Circles, clutches and clings
Clings to an innerness deeper than my heart
Clutches at 30 year old memories and stories
Circling in and out of time—

Time past; Time forgotten; Time remembered

The baby stretches out with hands overhead
Muscles unpracticed in utero—
Miracle of miracles
Seven days old.

On the flight home I remembered that my mother was completely anesthetized with each delivery, therefore she learned the sex of her babies from my dad. She often told me that my dad announced my birth by saying, "We have a beautiful baby daughter with her hands stretched above her head." My mother had often slept in the same position during her pregnancy.

I also recalled that one mid-morning over coffee my mother had asked my dad:

"Elmer, what was the happiest time of your life?" At 86 he answered: "When we brought the babies home." My mother had stayed in the hospital with each of her babies for two full weeks.

How fortunate all three of us were to come home to a father who loved us unconditionally all of our lives. In his later years, in spite of alcoholism and periodic depression, I was sure of his quick smile and enduring love.

Memories of long ago… . They remind me of how fortunate I was and still am to have had loving parents.

Looking forward to seeing you for breakfast tomorrow.

Love, mary

From: Carli, Ann
Sent: Sat 11/26/2005 10:02 a.m.
To: MaryScherr@aol.com
Subject: Happy News

Dear Mary,

I am fascinated with the small, seemingly insignificant memories that hold fast to consciousness, especially when "important" names and facts can disappear so easily. It's as if the intact memory is stored, waiting to emerge at the right time.

Years ago I sent a greeting card to a friend with this message:

"The second time you fall in love is with a grandchild."

Logan Alexander was born Thanksgiving Eve. I looked into his inkwell eyes and fell in love again.

Love, Ann

From: Scherr, Mary
Sent: Sun 11/26/2005 8:24 p.m.
To: ann_carli@yahoo.com
Subject: Congratulations

Dear Ann,

CONGRATULATIONS! I am so pleased that Logan has arrived. Wonderful timing to arrive right before Thanksgiving. And I completely understand how you fell in love the second time. My love to the Mother, Father, and Grandmother! Looking forward to seeing you soonish!

Love, mary

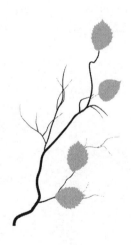

From: Carli, Ann
Sent: Thurs 12/8/2005 7:20 p.m.
To: MaryScherr@aol.com
Subject: Babies

Dear Mary,

I know you will understand the break in my communication. Your happiness for me with this new little boy is well founded. He is the tiny light in my firmament. I think of yet another parallel of our lives, lamenting that the beloved grandchild will never know the beloved grandfather.

I want to go back to your letter of 11/19 and the tender poem you wrote of your early morning communion with newborn Derek. The entire poem is very beautiful, capturing the wonderment and love surrounding an infant. The story of your father's happiest memory at 86 "bringing the babies home" made me cry.

When I learned my first grandchild was to be a girl, Lydia, I too wrote a poem, "Awhirl!" The title was an exuberant play on words and expression of joy. I'll paste it at the end of this letter. You can hear in the tone that my granddaughter poem was written at a very different time in my life.

Awhirl!

Awhirl
Blown dandelion fairy wands
Awhirl, awhirl
Pinwheels and ferris wheels
Awhirl
Tricycle spokes
Awhirl, awhirl
Splashes of paint, bursts of song
Awhirl
Maple leaves
Awhirl
Book pages
Awhirl, awhirl
Sea spray and sandcastles
Awhirl, awhirl, awhirl
Potters wheels, fishing reels
Awhirl
Dancing skirts
Awhirl, awhirl
In love
Awhirl

And now I feel another surge of life prompting a very different image and another irresistible play on words for my tiny grandboy, Logan:

Ahoy, Ahoy!

Tiny skiff
abreast your mother ship,
riding out squalls and swells.
So many voyages ahead.
If only I could secure
your mainsail,
guarantee translucent skies,
skim sailing
and an ever-protected harbor.

But winds and waves
will test your hull,
the blazing sun will sear,
fog obscure your way,
and tempests change your course.

When all is dark,
horizon clouded,
chart and compass blurred,
behold the sky
and find the brightest star
to bring you safely home.

Love, Ann

Winter

From: Scherr, Mary
Sent: Sun 12/18/2005 5:19 p.m.
To: ann_carli@yahoo.com
Subject: Reflecting on Decembers

Dear Ann,

I love the playful joyousness of "Awhirl!" for a girl and the quieter but equally loving tribute to your new sailor.

Now, as the days grow shorter and holidays approach, I suspect that for both of us painful memories can momentarily block out a myriad of happy ones.

A year ago you were aware that Angelo's illness was terminal... as all around you friends and neighbors were preparing for parties and special dinners. Five years ago Stu was lying unconscious in an Acute Care Unit.

We had been looking forward to both of our daughters and their families being home for Christmas. The last day of his life we shopped, had lunch together, and decided to spend the evening at home. I fell asleep that night listening to Stu play the clarinet, in preparation for an upcoming concert.

Shortly after midnight, Stu's loud, strange breathing woke me up. Thinking he was snoring I tapped his shoulder, "Stu, Stu." No response. He was unconscious. And never regained consciousness. So I like to think that he died in his sleep in his own bed.

Two days after being on life support, we had to make a wrenching decision. On Christmas day, when Cynthia and Janet and I were all at the hospital, Jerry, our minister, arrived. We talked through the decision of when or whether to remove life support. Originally we were advised that if he recovered within 24 hours, his chances were good, if later, he could become a vegetable. We knew the documents he had signed stated "No heroic measures," yet deciding to withdraw support was excruciatingly painful. Fortunately we were supported gently, sensitively, but clearly by our minister. Stu died the next morning on Sunday.

Our minister and his wife came to our house right after church to help us plan the memorial service. We decided at that time to have an unveiling ceremony one year later in accordance with Jewish practice.

Considering the painful December experiences etched in my memory forever, I find it remarkable that the holiday seasons have had many joyful moments. Time does transmute emotions toward feelings of gratitude for a life lovingly shared.

Love, mary

From: Carli, Ann
Sent: Tues 12/20/2005 9:26 p.m.
To: MaryScherr@aol.com
Subject: Re: Reflecting on Decembers

Dear Mary,

I so appreciate your reliving the last days of
Stu's life with me. They seemed to encompass the
supreme joys of living and ultimate sadness of a
good life ending.

I remember seeing you both at Pam's Christmas
party maybe a day or two before. Stu was in a
festive mood and we chatted about "the kids" as
we always did. I also think he told me about the
book group he was enjoying. Wasn't he the only
man in the group? I am grateful for that sweet,
brief memory of him.

I am struck by the anticipation you and Stu
shared that last day, looking forward to the family's
holiday together, shopping together, the two of
you having lunch, and then making the decision to
spend the evening at home. What a perfect day!

From midnight on, however, your life changed
forever and this lifetime of love you had created
closed its circle. I believe with you his last
moments were there beside you in the bed you had
shared for forty years. I think he had left his body
to close down.

No one can know the strength and courage you and your daughters had to find to follow through on Stu's wishes. It does seem to me, however, that if one is open to wisdom, it comes and we can do what is right and good. You three were wise and good and right in your careful, loving support of this good man's request of you.

Love, Ann

From: Scherr, Mary
Sent: Thurs 12/22/2005 11:19 PM
To: ann_carli@yahoo.com
Subject: Off to Palm Springs

Dear Ann,

I'm leaving with Carol for Palm Springs early tomorrow morning. I find it easier to do something very different for Christmas. The weather will be warm, the pool relaxing, and avoiding the mounds of packages that take forever to open—will be good! I'll come home on the 26th and leave the next day for Oregon. I do want to spend time with Cynth and family while Derek and Kathryn are on winter break.

I'll be thinking of you and hoping all goes well. Take good care of yourself and enjoy Logan's first Christmas!

Love, mary

From: Carli, Ann
Sent: Fri 12/23/2005 12:55 a.m.
To: MaryScherr@aol.com
Subject: Christmas

Dear Mary,

You probably won't check your e-mail before leaving today so may not read this until your return from Palm Springs. I did want to write tonight (this morning really), and tell you I appreciated continuing our Champagne Gathering again this year at Pam's last night. I had to take a deep breath as I arrived because I had not seen Jackie or Nicole since last year's party when I remembered slipping out of the house for a short while as Angelo was sleeping. The days were dwindling down to a precious few, as in "September Song," one of my favorite songs—especially sung by Walter Huston a thousand years ago. What different meaning it has now.

I do hope you have an "unusually" different and good Christmas!

Love, Ann

From: Scherr, Mary
Sent: Mon 1/2/2006 3:11 p.m.
To: ann_carli@yahoo.com
Subject: Christmas and New Year's

Dear Ann,

The holidays are always difficult for widows and widowers—and according to counselors, the contrast between media extravagances of jubilant, merry, beautiful people in beautiful houses and the reality causes serious depression for some.

I did long for the laughter, music, and ringing of phones so typical of holidays when the house was full. I now find it easier to do something very different. Christmas in the desert was definitely different. No last minute dashes to the grocery store or midnight stuffing of stockings. The weather was warm, the pool delightful, and the rotating tram up the mountain was fun. Carol and I gave each other little packages that were useful, fun, or consumable!

We followed dinner recommendations from friends for "must go to" restaurants. The morning after dining in the most elegant and most expensive of the restaurants, Carol confided that she really didn't enjoy big expensive meals with more food that we wished. I knew I didn't either! We both think Christmas is far too commercial and materialistic—

but we had followed the suggestions of others and the convention of patronizing one of the "best" places to eat.

I thoroughly enjoyed my visit to Oregon—all grandmothers think their grandchildren are the brightest, best looking, and most fun, but mine really, truly are!

I planned to get home for a New Year's Dinner party with close friends but Midwest weather disrupted air traffic for two days. I finally arrived home New Year's Eve at 11:50 PM, via a cab from the airport, walked thru the kitchen directly to the garage, drove to the party, honked loudly at 11:55 just in time for an exuberant welcome and a New Year's toast with very close friends.

The year 2006 will be rewarding and stimulating and deeply satisfying—although different, but life changes every year and is always filled with potential. That's my commercial for the new year.

Love, mary

From: Carli, Ann
Sent: Mon 1/2/2006 11:17 p.m.
To: MaryScherr@aol.com
Subject: Holidays

Dear Mary,

Your holidays were filled with dear old friends
and brand new friends. I loved hearing all the
details. Like you, I wanted to do something totally
different at Christmas. In reality, I wanted to do
nothing—no tree, no special dinners, no Christmas
morning gift extravaganza. But this was Logan's
first Christmas and I did not want to undermine
that with Sabrina. And my niece was very eager
to come from Berkeley and see the baby. She and
her husband have joined us for many Christmases
and, again, I did not want to disappoint her. So
I went by myself and bought the six-foot tree,
stuffed it in the car, hauled it in the house, dragged
the lights out, with my spirits dragging further
and further behind. I decided my one act of
rebellion would be the ornaments. I didn't want to
put up our traditional family ornaments. So I went
out and bought new ones, all monochromatic, like
my spirit. After completely decorating the tree,
half the lights went out. At that point I wanted to
throw the whole thing out and run away. Philip

called from New York in the midst of my ennui and firmly told me I could not throw out the tree. So everything came off, new lights went on, decorations were replaced.

If this were an O. Henry story, it would end with my rediscovering the true meaning of Christmas by stumbling upon some symbol or sign. But this is not an O. Henry story. We had the tree, the special meals, the Christmas morning gift extravaganza, but there was no enlightenment.

It was not that Christmas was any harder than any other day this past year. I just didn't want to do it. To me, the holidays were just days, no sadder than the 10th of October, the 26th of September, the 6th of August, etc., etc. I have tried to explain this to friends. My reality is that being at the absolute bottom of heartache, there is nowhere further down to go. I can't miss Angelo any more on Christmas than any other day. I think it is important that people realize there are many different ways to grieve and many different ways to rearrange one's life after the death of a loved one. There is no formula, pattern, or schematic. I really want to know how others manage because I know each reality is unique. Your reality has been helpful to me. I have so appreciated reading your letters and have been grateful for the opportunity to reflect on them and respond.

As for resolutions, I hope to write more, learn something new, enroll in a class or workshop, work on my health, travel a little, contribute something worthwhile, and watch my grandson grow into his potential!

Love, Ann

From: Scherr, Mary
Sent: Wed 1/4/2006 8:02 a.m.
To: ann_carli@yahoo.com
Subject: Unveiling

Dear Ann,

My first Christmas without Stu was very difficult and was so much harder than other days. Both Cynth's and Janet's families were here for Christmas and for the unveiling service two days later that we had planned the previous year. Janet and Andrew, new parents with a new baby drove down from Glendale. Cynth, Bruce, Kathryn, and Derek flew down from Oregon. Cynth had mailed all the Santa presents. Her kids spent part of the time with their Dad's parents who live nearby. Logistic details multiplied throughout each day. All of us were edgy. I tried to neutralize conflicts and the stress of keeping raw emotions under control was exhausting. I remember very little else about Christmas that year.

At the time we planned Stu's memorial service, we decided to have an unveiling service a year later, in accordance with Jewish custom. With the help of Laurie, one of my former doctoral students, who is a rabbi, I had ordered a tomb stone with Stu's name in Hebrew, and arranged a service in which the headstone is unveiled at the cemetery.

We invited only relatives. Stu's brother, his wife, and son came from New York. His cousin and his wife came from Newport Beach, my daughters and their husbands were present along with a niece and a grandniece from San Diego.

Beautiful pink and cream-colored roses nestled in eucalyptus leaves covered the grave and one rose rested on each chair in the small circle around the gravesite. The rabbi is a special woman and I felt blessed to have her conduct the service. She read Hebrew blessings and together we read an English Kaddish. Everyone shared memories. I can't, however, remember anything.

After the service, we came home for lunch. We lit the memory candle to burn for 24 hours. Mal, Stu's cousin, said the Kaddish again in Hebrew and I felt connected to the 2,000 plus years of Stu's heritage.

The next day after everyone had left, I realized that the candle had burned for 24 hours. I should blow it out. I could not. I decided to wait until the next morning.

The next day I still could not extinguish the candle. I needed my own brief ritual. I read the English version of the Kaddish; I read a blessing found on the front page of the San Diego Jewish Times for December 2000. I cried.

Slowly I put clusters of rose petals from the centerpiece into a blue glass dish. With each of more than 30 clusters I named a "gift" from my life with Stu. I then read the blessing again. This time out loud to myself, asking for strength in the days ahead.

And I added a litany especially for Stu:

May your light, which blessed many of us,
Inspire me to find the courage and the strength
To lead a life which blesses others.
Amen and Shalom.

I then calmly blew out the candle.

The beautiful, graveside service embraced me with warmth and love. The very best part of that December. Sharing memories with you also nurtures and renews my commitment to live with courage and strength.

Love, mary

From: Carli, Ann
Sent: Wed 1/4/2006 10:13 p.m.
To: MaryScherr@aol.com
Subject: Re: Unveiling

Dear Mary,

I knew you were having a one-year remembrance ceremony but we never talked about it. I used to be perplexed by people who marked sad anniversaries, but now I understand. I confess I am not greatly drawn to symbolic gestures like doves flying, balloons with messages soaring, etc., but your family coming together simply with flowers feels so simple and pure.

Your personal ceremony and litany touched me deeply, Mary, and your spiritual responses are so very beautiful. I understand what you wrote about the great significance and connection of Hebrew history, traditions, and heritage. I am filled with a sense that somehow he was there with you and was gratified by your honoring him in these religious and symbolic ways, first with his family and then, later, alone as his life partner.

I think it must have had individual meaning and collective bonding for each of you to speak about your beloved husband, father, brother, brother-in-law, father-in-law, cousin.

As I have tried to adjust and reconcile myself to—even to believe—Angelo being gone, I have had tiny flashes of empathy for our son and daughter, our daughter-in-law and granddaughter; his sister, brother-in-law and nephews; my sister, brother-in-law, niece, and nephew; his friends and colleagues, all of whom are bereft of his uniqueness.

Your ceremonial tribute to Stu was a loving way to acknowledge not only his life but also his continuing place in each of your lives.

Love, Ann

From: Scherr, Mary
Sent: Thurs 1/12/2006 9:40 p.m.
To: ann_carli@yahoo.com
Subject: Etchings

Dear Ann,

Thank you for your comments regarding the unveiling ceremony. It seems like so many years ago, yet I do remember how helpful the ritual was at that time.

I miss Stu's reaction to life and his sensitivity that nearly always matched mine. Two decades ago, shortly before Christmas, Stu told me one of his patients wanted to show us his etchings of English cathedrals. The patient-artist arrived on Stu's day off, displayed eight or nine etchings, talked about each at length, mentioned the prices, wanted to know which ones we liked best and then strongly urged us to keep two for a couple of days to see how we liked them. As he was gathering up his art portfolios, I learned that his wife had been waiting in the car for nearly an hour. "Oh, she should have come in," I protested. "She never does when I am making a sales call," he explained. He left. Stu and I looked at each other in amazement. Stu had no idea he had arranged a private showing as a prelude to purchase. Although we thought the etchings were skillfully done, we didn't wish to own any of them. However, considering that it was the holiday season, considering that the artist thought we were interested in a purchase, and considering we should have anticipated his expectation, Stu thought we should buy one. We did. And we both felt comfortable with the decision. A few years later I donated the etching to the library.

As usual these e-mails exhibit a stream of consciousness. I don't know why thinking about the unveiling triggered thoughts of that Thursday afternoon looking at cathedral etchings. You, too, have written about how Angelo and you had the same reactions to many situations.

Love, mary

From: Carli, Ann
Sent: Fri 1/13/2006 4:22 p.m.
To: MaryScherr@aol.com
Subject: Residuals

Dear Mary,

One of the lovely residuals of our writing is
this "stream-of-consciousness" to which you refer. I
wasn't sure about that word "residual" so looked it
up to find the meaning, one of which is so pertinent:

Main Entry: ¹re·sid·u·al
Pronunciation: ri-'zi-jə-wəl, -jəl; -'zij-wəl
Function: noun
Etymology: Latin residuum residue
Something that remains after completion of process
  that involves the removal of part of the original.

Here we are sharing from our innermost core
what the "removal of part of the original"—our
phenomenal husbands—means to each of us, "after
the completion of process"—life and death.

So much does remain of Stu and Angelo. I am
resisting the word "memories" and want to say
instead the pieces of their lives that represented
what they were as human beings, what those pieces
meant to us at the time, and how they burrowed
into our consciousness to emerge and be present.

The piece about the "private showing" says so much about Stu's and your kindness, your collaborative approach to problem solving, your shared sense of humor! Don't you think those uncomfortable moments make the best stories of our lives?

It may be because we learn more from them than the happy vignettes, just as we learn more from mistakes than successes.

Thanks for the residuals!

Love, Ann

From: Scherr, Mary
Sent: Tues 1/24/2006 10:44 p.m.
To: ann_carli@yahoo.com
Subject: Re: Residuals

Dear Ann,

I love your analysis of "residuals." Much more meaningful than how I usually think of the word. I was perplexed by the intricacies of the "Residual Trust" created after Stu's death. I felt confused and incompetent. Feelings of incompetence contributed to a general sense of vulnerability without Stu. So residual did not conjure up any positive feelings although a residual trust for my daughters is indeed a positive financial asset and a definite reminder of how carefully and thoroughly Stu planned for our future.

I also acknowledge Stu's influence that remains—those pieces of his life "that meant so much to us at the time" and "burrowed into our consciousness to emerge and be present" still today. You expressed what I feel so effectively. Thank you.

I am grateful for this opportunity to share views with you as it has caused me to reflect on my life with Stu and acknowledge those reflections in words—a tangible residual as opposed to thoughts, which float in and out of consciousness. I like the words.

Love, mary

My Brief Biographical Sketch of Stuart Norman Scherr

    Stuart's grandparents on both sides of the family were immigrants from Russia and Austria. His maternal grandfather had a successful tailor shop in Manhattan, but wanted to move out of the city after he witnessed a friend injured by a horse-drawn wagon. He boarded the eastern-bound train and went as far away from the city as he could go and still be in an area where he could walk to the shul on the Jewish Sabbath. He chose New Rochelle as the place to raise his four sons and two daughters, one of whom was Stuart's mother. Following the tradition of many immigrants, the eldest son worked his way through college and then helped his three younger brothers. All four sons became attorneys. Stuart's mother worked as a legal stenographer. Neither she nor her sister attended college. Sending daughters to college was not part of the tradition.

    Stuart's parents spent the first few years of their marriage in Brooklyn, where Stuart was born, but the family soon moved to New Rochelle, where his father co-owned a drug store. After attending public schools, Stuart graduated from Oberlin College and Cornell Medical School and then served two years as a Navy medical officer. During his last assignment he was stationed at the Navy hospital at Camp Pendleton.

    Mary was teaching English at Claremont High School in San Diego and met her future husband at an officer's club, where a lot of school teachers and bachelor Navy officers enrolled in classes ostensibly to learn new dance steps but actually to meet potential dates. They met in March 1959, married in June and flew to New York where Stuart began residency in Internal Medicine at the Upstate Medical University in Syracuse.

So a protestant school teacher from California and a Jewish doctor from New York began a married life that lasted 40 years.

For 31 of those years Stuart practiced internal medicine in Oceanside, California regularly working 11-13 hour days. A major heart attack forced him to retire years before he had planned. During retirement he attended hospital board and committee meetings and spoke strongly in favor of Tri-City Medical Center remaining public. He played clarinet in two community orchestras and volunteered as a docent at the San Diego Botanical Gardens (formerly Quail Botanical Gardens). Most important of all, he had time to spend with children and two grandchildren. He was delighted to learn that another granddaughter was expected in spring.

He also had time to appreciate and relish his daily environment. Stu heard the song of a non-resident bird in the yard, took pictures of baby owls, saw reflections in windows and took photos of patterns in the beach sand. His deep appreciation of the beauty of nature and his reverence for life are valued legacies.

From: Carli, Ann
Sent: Thurs 1/26/2006 11:48 p.m.
To: MaryScherr@aol.com
Subject: The World Around Me

Dear Mary,

Here is another of those experiences I struggle with. This evening, a friend dropped by to return some dishes to me. She was en route to a business dinner and mentioned that she had been out every night this week and that she and her husband hadn't had a dinner during this period. "Does he get take out?" I asked. "I don't know," she replied, "I haven't asked." When she saw the expression on my face she anxiously said, "Should I?" I just smiled and mumbled some reassurance. But my heart was aching.

I hope you will hear this as my emotional, rather than judgmental, response. Angelo and I both had careers that kept us on the run and we too would have periods of not being home at night. But we always caught up with each other, checked up on each other, cared about what the other had done, eaten, seen. It was part of being connected. I know so many couples that live lives of disquiet separation. It is painful for me to observe. I feel as if I have unjustifiably been sentenced to life imprisonment while the guilty continue freely with their lives.

I needed to share this with someone tonight.

Love, Ann

From: Scherr, Mary
Sent: Thurs 2/2/2006 10:03 p.m.
To: ann_carli@yahoo.com
Subject: Connection and Separation

Dear Ann,

Ann, I am sorry that I am just now reading your letter—"a sad one"—because I would have liked to have responded quickly. My reaction was complex. I understand why, I think, your heart was aching for your friend since you and Angelo stayed in touch and knew how a relationship stays close. And yes, I did read it as an emotional response and not judgmental.

About 15 years ago, I attended a workshop given by a husband and wife psychiatrist team from the Stone Center at Wellesley College (Janet Surrey and Steve Bergman). The subject was relationships. I recall during the concluding session that Bergman stressed that when one spouse called the other during the workday it was important to indicate pleasure in your voice and state a time when you could talk. He felt busy couples often received calls at inconvenient times, and could say: "It's good to hear from you. Could we talk at 5:30? I'll call you then." Suggesting a time rather than stating curtly: "I can't talk now." I was impressed and wanted to do that. It did not happen.

Stu did not want any phone calls at work. I probably called him less than a dozen times in 30 years. He called to say when he thought he'd be home— (usually estimating an hour or two earlier than he arrived). His situation was, however, different. He almost always ate at the hospital on workdays. When I said: "Some doctors come home to eat dinner with their families and then go back to the hospital," he retorted: "Some doctors prefer to make rounds on patients when they are asleep. I want to talk with patients." End of conversation. He knew how he wanted to practice medicine and that was it.

Stu rarely called me at work. When I was on campus I was usually in class or meeting with students. I preferred to do paperwork at home. Just a couple weeks before he died, he called me at my office before I had to leave for class. His voice was jubilant. He wanted me to know that Janet had been to her doctor, the baby was fine, she was expecting a girl, and the doctor felt sure she would carry this one. He was absolutely delighted—as was I.

After the relational workshop, we did make one change. We decided that when one of us returned home on his day off or on weekends, we would find the other (in house or yard, even practicing clarinet!) and greet each other warmly and enthusiastically! It took practice (I didn't like interruptions when reading papers; he didn't like interruptions when practicing) but we did succeed and felt it made a big difference. To come home and not make contact felt very empty.

After Stu retired, he always had dinner ready when I came home or else we went out.

So, I agree that it is very sad to observe a "disquiet separation." Another indication that your marriage was special, so related, so close that I can't find adequate words. Do we suppose that those who lead far more separate lives experience less of a loss? I suspect they may feel regret over not experiencing a marriage similar to yours.

I'm glad you shared. Looking forward to talking to you tonight, so we can make plans to see each other.

Gotta go read resumes—we are in the midst of a search process.

Love, mary

From: Carli, Ann
Sent: Fri 2/3/2006 9:17 a.m.
To: MaryScherr@aol.com
Subject: Relationships

Dear Mary,

Thank you for really hearing my sadness for my friend's marriage as well as my sadness for my own truly wonderful marriage now ended.

Of course I realize that Stu as a physician and you as a professor in a classroom would have a different system of communication. Angelo and I had the unusual professional freedom as well as our personal desire to stay connected during the day. We usually talked at least once a day at work, if only to say, "I'm on my way home."

How wonderful that you and Stu could implement the idea of a new and meaningful coming home to each other! How very, very wonderful. Yes, we were both exceptionally fortunate, Mary. I am so grateful.

Love, Ann

From: Scherr, Mary
Sent: Tues 2/14/2006 11:58 p.m.
To: ann_carli@yahoo.com
Subject: Evolving relationships

Dear Ann,

In your last e-mail you wrote how wonderful that Stu and I could implement a "meaningful coming home." True, but it happened after many years of marriage—in fact, I think we most successfully implemented that ritual after he retired! For three plus decades he came home after me. When he retired, I frequently came home to find his car already in the garage and I felt a spurt of energy and pleasure and wanted to find him immediately.

Marriages do evolve. Relationships become increasingly meaningful if two people share needs, pleasures, and concerns.

I think both of my daughters have far more emotional insight than I did at their age. And I think they are aware of their own emotions to a degree neither Stu nor I were in the first decades of our marriage.

For many years I often kept my emotions in check. I was so much more spontaneous than Stu who had an almost stern, work-oriented streak. He didn't allow himself much playfulness except with the girls or after he had been on vacation for a few days and gradually relaxed. I didn't express my wilder enthusiasms with him as I didn't want them dampened, or rationalized away. Fortunately I had children and friends who appreciated what one called my "well preserved sense of child."

I never told Stu that his put-downs, however clever, were hurtful. I shared one of his early morning comments with my therapist: "Are you going to let her wear that?" Stu asked as one of the girls arrived at the breakfast table. My therapist laughed and said, "That's surely a double put-down."

He was witty, however, had a wide array of interests, and I was never ever bored with him. In addition, I trusted and respected him and was proud to be his wife. When I left home to work on a doctoral degree and was out of town 3-4 days at a time, he was completely supportive and took over most aspects of house maintenance, including grocery shopping and bill paying—and did so without any complaints. His rationality in those cases rescued me from ambivalence. "I don't think we'll be able to keep the plants on the deck alive when I'm gone so much," I mused. "What do you think it would cost to replace them all?" he asked. We both laughed. That cost would be completely negligible.

Over the years he mellowed and I gradually learned to share my feelings as well as my thoughts. In retrospect, I was fortunate to have a brilliant, perceptive therapist thirty-five years ago who helped me get in touch with my own needs and helped me understand Stu.

Oh, my how the thoughts do flow. It is nearly midnight. Let's talk soon and arrange a breakfast.

Love, mary

From: Carli, Ann
Sent: Thurs 2/16/2006 7:22 p.m.
To: MaryScherr@aol.com
Subject: Marriage

Dear Mary,

It seems like these are short stories that make up your anthology. Stu's legacy at Tri-City Hospital is a heroic one. There could be one, which might be titled "His Children." I've often thought that Angelo's children were different from my children, taking into consideration the gender differences and dynamics, temperament, and parenting styles.

It's taken us a while to discuss what components we think made up our unusually happy marriages. I agree that sustained relationships evolve. I think this is true in friendship as well as marriage, and of course the best marriages are the best friendships. I used to think of this evolution as shifting gears where both people must willingly shift to the next stage, sometimes struggling up the hills and sometimes coasting down, the occasional unexpected downward shift—a process that progresses and stalls and sometimes goes backwards.

I think that Angelo's and my similar family backgrounds were important factors in our marriage. Our parents were all immigrants, his from Italy, and mine from England and Canada. We both came from working class families and were the first in our families to go to college.

A high school teacher gave memorable advice to our class that before marriage people should spend time with each other's family. I don't know why it made an impression on me but I always remembered this and it worked out that Angelo and I did just that. He knew he was marrying into a family disjointed by an alcoholic father. I knew I was the non-Italian, non-Catholic, West Coast girl who was stealing their prince away.

To me shared values were the most important factors in our marriage. Loyalty was foremost for us. We put our family first in our lives. We supported each other's work but it was the means to the end. We agreed on money, though Angelo was the saver and I was the spender. He would say he would have never traveled except for me and I would say we would have no savings except for him. He never cared about material things but appreciated our home, the garden, the clothes I bought for him. He was tolerant of my weekend trips to the nurseries and I was tolerant of the boxes of books he would stack in the garage. We had both mutual and separate interests and friends. Although our parenting styles were different, he being the more conservative parent, we stood united to our children on important decisions. We married in the Catholic Church but he soon fell away, confirming his family's fears. One year I dragged the family to various churches, trying to find a fit. We never did. The kids would roll their eyes as we drove up to a new church. Angelo and I did discuss philosophy continuously. Usually on Sunday mornings, now that I think of it. Ironic.

We learned over the years to communicate honestly and respectfully, even when angry with each other. I think just when we got our life together really right, it ended.

Love, Ann

From: Scherr, Mary
Sent: Tues 2/21/2006 9:51 p.m.
To: ann_carli@yahoo.com
Subject: Mixed marriages

Dear Ann,

Stu and I knew that spending time with each other's family was a good idea, but we sure didn't follow that advice. We knew each other a little over two months when we planned to marry. Stu met my parents for the first time on a Saturday night in June when we announced we were getting married in three weeks. Stu's parents were shocked that he was getting married on the West Coast as they were expecting him back in New York in less than a month to begin residency at Update Medical Center in Syracuse.

One of Stu's aunts thought it far more reasonable for us to be engaged, but being 3,000 miles apart during a residency schedule did not make any sense to Stu and he wouldn't consider it. Five days after he phoned his parents he received the following:

Dear Stuart,

To us you are very dear
For your future we have fear,
The stage is all set.
You are in the net
Your love must stand the test of time
Or else it isn't worth a dime.
Set an engagement date
And then wait! Wait! Wait!
If your love is phony
You pay alimony!
One marriage out of four
They end up as before.
This is the truth
From your loving

Aunt Ruth

We thought the poem was hilariously funny. From this vantage point, I consider it rather reasonable. Stu had been raised as a conservative Jew. I was Protestant. We were contemplating a "mixed marriage," as it was known in those days. In spite of the surprise, shock, and reservations on Stu's side of the family, his parents and brother flew out from New York for the wedding.

The day of the wedding my mother broke a jelly glass. Stu's Dad thought that was a promising sign since a wine glass is broken in a Jewish service. We wanted both a minister and a rabbi to marry us but the rabbi said we'd have to be married in temple. Instead we were married in my parents' living room by my inclusive-minded minister, who revised the traditional marriage ceremony to replace "Christians" with "Children of God" and omitted any reference to a triune God.

Let me know your schedule so we can meet.

Love, mary

From: Carli, Ann
Sent: Wed 2/22/2006 10:27 p.m.
To: MaryScherr@aol.com
Subject: Re: Mixed marriages

Dear Mary,

"The Truth from Aunt Ruth" made me laugh, too! This is yet another similarity in our lives, Mary—marrying someone from another faith into a family not thrilled with the prospect. I wonder if there is research on the success rate of marriages that overcome family opposition because of different religions, races, ages, social class. I'd like to think they are more successful than homogenous partnerships—a testimony of love and a test of character—sort of a "we'll show you."

We also had opposition from the young Catholic priest who gave me the requisite "instructions." He obviously was displeased with our engagement. He asked Angelo when the wedding was and when he heard it was six months away, he said to Angelo, "Oh, then you have time to change your mind!" This was said in front of me. Fortunately, a different elderly priest married us. Angelo's best man, his cousin, reported the priest said quietly to him "these two are going to stay married."

Love, Ann

From: Scherr, Mary
Sent: Mon 3/5/2006 8:20 a.m.
To: ann_carli@yahoo.com
Subject: Elderly Wisdom

Dear Ann,

Thank goodness for an elderly priest who was both sensitive and wise. Those were the days when neither Protestants nor Catholics encouraged mixed marriages. I recall reading a pamphlet from my church entitled "If I marry a Roman Catholic." My minister pointed out I'd give up my right to choose how I wanted to raise my children. But as we know couples married and made their own decisions.

Love, mary

From: Carli, Ann
Sent: Wed 3/7/2006 10:47 p.m.
To: MaryScherr@aol.com
Subject: Anger

Dear Mary,

When Angelo died my sister suggested I
would go through a phase being angry at Angelo
for dying. I assume she was hearkening back to
the formulas that therapists outlined for grief. I
told her I could not imagine feeling anger toward
Angelo. He didn't want to die. And he certainly
didn't want to leave me with all the complications
of his "collections"—the storage unit filled to the
gunnels with his stuff, the 10,000 books filling up
our garage and his study. As often as I shook my
head wondering, "What was he thinking???" and
as hard as the sorting out and divestiture has been,
I have never felt anger towards him.

Tonight, however, I am angry. I am angry
toward others about their assumptions in regards
to his death. Today is Angelo's birthday. He would
have been 69. Three people asked me what was
I going to do or what did I do on this hard day. I
wanted to scream, "Every day is a hard day. His
birthday is no different than any other day without
him." But, instead, I quietly explain this.

I am tired of people presuming they know what I feel, what I want, what I will or will not do, and, perhaps, what I should do. Of course I woke up thinking about him—as I do every morning. I wore my locket with his picture, as I do most days. I talked with him and listened for his response. I sent flowers to his sister as I did the previous year because it was a loving gesture that would have made him very happy. And tomorrow I will wake up thinking about him, see his smiling face in photos throughout the house, talk to him again, and listen for his guidance. I will send his sister an Easter card because he would have appreciated my reaching out to her.

What I would have appreciated is the friend who wrote and the other friend and his sister who called simply saying, "I am thinking about Angelo today, his birthday." That would have been enough. Can we add that to our list of "What to say" suggestions?

I may have already shared this poem with you. I wrote it on the anniversary of his death. The last two lines say it all:

Just Another Day

They write and call, remembering the date,
Projecting how sad it must be,
Like Christmas or your birthday:
"I know this is a difficult time for you"
They say, but they do not.
Because I am stubborn and perverse,
I will not acquiesce.
In each exchange I persevere again:
"This day is no harder than the others;
December 25 does not hurt more
Than September 9th, October 22nd.
They're all the same."
Because there's no way down from bottom,
And there's no time worse than now.
And, of course, you are the only one
Who would have understood.

Love, Ann

From: Scherr, Mary
Sent: Fri 3/8/2006 10:51 p.m.
To: ann_carli@yahoo.com
Subject: Re: Anger

Dear Ann,

Your poem is sad and effective. I think there is
a need for us to be as authentic and honest and
straightforward as possible. I make it a point to use
the word "died." Not "I lost my husband" or "my
husband has been gone for six years."

In regard to anger—one friend whose husband
had died told me that a divorced friend of hers said:
"I could be angry as hell at my husband; you can only
be angry at God." I thought that was really strange. I
couldn't relate at all.

Someone once tried to gently suggest I was
repressing my anger. That kind of dichotomous
thinking does anger me. There are not just two
reactions. And yet people try to be helpful by
spreading the popular idea that death causes anger
and it is best to acknowledge it.

When you wrote that friends remembered the
anniversary of Angelo's death and his birthday,
I thought how heartwarming. I can understand,
however, your preference for someone saying: "I am
thinking of Angelo today, his birthday." That would

have been sufficient and then no one would have assumed anything re: your reaction.

I'd have been pleased if my daughters and/or close friend remembered Stu's birthday or our anniversary. Fortunately, we had the unveiling a year after his memorial service and the presence of the entire family was wonderfully loving and supportive. I suspect that my daughters think it would be sad for me to have them remember Stu's birthday. Oh, my— difficult to know.

On Wednesday I met with one of my graduate students whose mother died three weeks ago. They brought her home from the hospital in accordance with her mother's wishes and the wishes of her family. (A nurse told me she never knew anyone who wanted to die in a hospital, but often the family didn't want the patient to die at home. I didn't know that.) During the final hours of her mother's life the entire family circled her bed and sang her favorite Hindu chants and prayers. Her father held her mother's hand for hours at a time.

My young student believes her mother has been released from this life and from her body and now is a free spirit at one with all creation. She has studied and read extensively the sacred scriptures from several wisdom traditions. Although she's my research assistant, she is my tutor. I'm glad you can come to my open house on the 26th. She and her father plan to come. Take care,

Love, mary

From: Carli, Ann
Sent: Sun 3/12/2006 9:17 a.m.
To: MaryScherr@aol.com
Subject: Remembering

Dear Mary,

I've been thinking about your wish that your daughters would remember Stu's birthday. This is an easy wish to fulfill. Tell them! Yes, they have busy lives but I know they would want to reach out in this way. As you suggest, they may have a misperception that it would be painful for you, rather than comforting. Even a message on voicemail "Thinking about Dad today" would be welcome, wouldn't it? Philip and Sabrina have let me know they remember Angelo on his birthday. This exchange with you prompts me to tell them this is important to me.

Do you remember the song, "These Foolish Things (Remind Me of You)"? Every day is filled with reminders of Angelo—glimpsing a red truck, tasting some wonderful food, hearing Billie Holiday or anything by Puccini or, especially, Masagni's "Intermezzo;" spotting grammatical errors which drove him crazy; sitting on the patio with coffee, etc., etc. The experience brings tears to my eyes but I cherish every connection.

I loved the account of your Hindu friend's family gathering, sharing, and singing around the mother as she died. This seems the perfect goodbye to me.

Love, Ann

From: Scherr, Mary
Sent: Sun 3/12/2006 10:42 p.m.
To: ann_carli@yahoo.com
Subject: "I" language

Dear Ann,

You pointed out that my suggestions, "Just say, 'I am glad to see you' or 'I've been thinking of you'" are "I" statements. I never made that connection even though I have heard many times that "I" language is better than "You" statements. Goes to show how hard it is for me to integrate that suggestion into daily life. Your counseling background is a major plus. And writing about this will make it easier for me to remember the "I" language, I think, I hope.

Your suggestion that I tell my kids I'd like them to remember Stu's birthday is great. I'll tell them I'd like them to acknowledge our anniversary, too! This brief exchange illustrates how important and helpful our exchanges have been and I am grateful.

I will check my work schedule tomorrow when I am on campus and then I can suggest possible days for us to get together.

Love to you and Sabrina and Logan—and I hope all is a bit better.

Love, mary

From: Carli, Ann
Sent: Wed 3/15/2006 9:28 p.m.
To: MaryScherr@aol.com
Subject: Decisions and Convictions

Dear Mary,

In a previous letter you wrote, "When one of
my kids said last year that I had trouble making
decisions, I was shocked. Then I realized that I did
procrastinate, was uncertain, because I was used
to input." This resonated with me, Mary. I think
the forty-plus years we shared with husbands who
would really listen, had meaningful opinions, and
were able to process with us made for wonderful
synergy. I too feel at a loss because I no longer have
Angelo to validate, veto, or improve upon an idea.
I now need to take more time in decision-making.
My natural tendency was to jump in and see how
things go. Angelo would temper this, adding a
much needed rational analysis. I feel insecure for
the first time in forty-three years.

I continuously dialogue with him, e.g., "What
should I do here?" I always get encouraging words
like "You're doing fine" or "You can do this."
I've also suggested this to Philip, who often gets
stuck in emotional reactions that do not serve
him well. I have said to him repeatedly this year:

"Ask yourself, what would Dad do? You will hear the right guidance." Although I would like to believe this is a spiritual connection, I think it is the permanent impression that Angelo left on his children and me.

I envy people who have conviction that there is more than this life. I am open to all possibilities but no longer seek them.

Love, Ann

Spring

From: Scherr, Mary
Sent: Sat 3/25/2006 8:33 a.m.
To: ann_carli@yahoo.com
Subject: Spiritual practice

Dear Ann,

I've been thinking a lot about the last paragraph that you wrote. I've concluded that those of us who do not have a firm, clear conviction of what comes after this life, have an advantage. We ponder, we think deeply, we wonder, and we may explore various spiritual traditions. Gradually we create our own authentic, individual response to life that resonates with our own beliefs and values.

Spirituality for me means "a way of being in the world in the light of the Mystery at the core of the universe." A definition by Maria Harris, to which I have added "and a way of living in the light of the need for justice and peace." I embrace, accept, and appreciate the mystery at the core of the universe. I see mystery everywhere. I don't understand how my body has the ability to heal a simple cut. How do cells receive instructions to respond to a particular spot on my wrist? How can a tiny dark seed include instructions for size, color of leaves, and elaborate flower designs? How can the universe be continually expanding?

I go to the ocean. I feel eternity spreads out before me. I feel a part of this creation. And I believe humans have a creative center that they can access. Nearly all of the world's spiritual traditions advise us to be still and listen to the voice of the creator, the creative force, or God.

A Jewish Sabbath prayer begins: "In this moment of quiet communion with Thee, oh Lord, a still small voice speaks in the depth of my spirit."

St. Augustine suggests that if we fall silent, we can hear the very voice of the Creator who made us and not just the words of His creation.

And a Hindu sacred text urges us to listen to the voice that constantly comes from within.

The modern saints, Dalai Lama, Bishop Tutu, Nelson Mandela, who have contributed to a more just and peaceful world, all have a strong spiritual foundation.

I plan to strengthen my spiritual practices, which require both discipline and patience. I need meditation to guide me toward more compassion and more commitment to work for justice and peace. Yet Theresia, who accepts dangerous volunteer assignments from the World Health Organization tells me meditation makes her "nervous." She doesn't meditate, she acts!

So… that reminds me there are individual paths! See you tomorrow.

Love, mary

From: Carli, Ann
Sent: Sun 3/27/2006 2:06 p.m.
To: MaryScherr@aol.com
Subject: More on Convictions

Dear Mary,

I was so impressed to meet your friend,
Theresia, and listen to her life story. She appeared
beatific as she described her work all over the
world. I am thinking about her courage and
strength in surviving in a prisoner of war camp,
her great love and great loss of her husband, her
fortitude and dedication in helping others. And to
think she is eighty years old!

I am also wondering if those elements of
character I perceived in her represent a truly good
life. So much is questioned, said, and written about
"the meaning of life." It occurs to me perhaps
we should instead examine what constitutes the
goodness of life. As I said, I am thinking...

Thank you for including me in your group of
interesting colleagues, students, and friends. It was
an extraordinary afternoon.

I so appreciate your sharing your beliefs with
me. I have to say I was stopped by your sentence
"I've concluded that those of us who do not have
a firm, clear conviction of what comes after this
life, have an advantage" because I perceive you as

having such conviction. Your following statements about mystery, eternity, and creative force reinforce my perception. Yet, at the same time, I do hear you are exploring and working toward commitment through spiritual practice. I suppose my perception emanates from contrasting what I see as your connection to my disconnection. I have often said I envy people who have faith. I do understand the concept, perhaps even the experience of faith, but it is a concept and experience outside of my reality. I imagine how protected one must feel to be so sure of religious teachings and convinced a messiah or prophet was divine. So, you see, I wonder if the "advantage" is theirs.

In regards to convictions, I enjoyed creating a vocabulary lesson to teach my English as Second Language students the words "think," "know," "wonder," "hope," "imagine," and "believe." My students are from Oaxaca and work in the flower and strawberry fields. Each Tuesday evening after a long day in the field they come to learn English for two hours. For this session we created sentences together to demonstrate the differences in vocabulary for thinking, e.g., wishing, wondering, knowing, understanding. When I offered the example for believing, "Many people believe in God," one of my favorite, very sensitive students, Archangel, said softly, "Anna, do you believe in

God?" I was so pleased at his courage in asking me and knew I had to answer truthfully. After a moment of thought, I replied, "Archangel, I hope there is a God."

God or no god, I do believe we are all parts of a system where one part affects all the others. Some call it the ripple effect or butterfly effect or "sensitive dependence on initial conditions," as put forth by Edward Lorenz. And, yes, I do hear the irony in my belief of connectedness while I myself feel so disconnected myself. But remember what I said to Archangel!

Hopefully, Ann

From: Scherr, Mary
Sent: Sun 4/2/2006 4:20 p.m.
To: ann_carli@yahoo.com
Subject: Hope

Dear Ann,

I'm so pleased to learn of your "hope." But first I need to respond to the first part of your e-mail.

I do have a firm, clear conviction that there is more to this life than is readily apparent because of the great mystery all around us.

Now back to your hope! Erik Erikson reminds us that "'hope" seems to be related to "hop" which means "leap." We often hear the expression "a leap of faith." For me, hop connotes playfulness perhaps because of the game of hopscotch. And I associate playfulness with creativity. You have so much creativity and so much to contribute that I am deeply pleased that you are leaning toward hope. Otherwise, most of us are overwhelmed by the unspeakable horrors happening in the world.

And now it's my turn to turn to the dictionary.

Hope: verb,"to long for with expectation of obtainment."
Hope: noun, Erikson describes 'hope' as "expectant desire."

So, I hope (verb) my future days are lived with meaning and I do have hope (noun).

Playfully and with love, mary

From: Carli, Ann
Sent: Mon 4/3/2006 9:58 a.m.
To: MaryScherr@aol.com
Subject: Re: Hope

Dear Mary,

You are indeed playful! I think you are
wonderful to have this winsome approach to living.
You give positive energy to those around you.

I fear I have lost most of my free spirit. My little
grandson does inspire me to be free and silly but
when I am not with him my world turns into a
quiet and serious place.

I like Erikson's relating hope and hop.
Webster's definition of hope brings to mind
one of my favorite aphorisms: "Live with no
expectations but great expectancy." I think that is
a hopeful statement.

Do you know Abraham Maslow's hierarchy of
needs? His outline of what people need to become
self-actualizing has been significant in my life. I
used to teach this every semester in my Women's
Studies classes so students could assess their own
needs and understand others. I had such a clear
understanding of what Maslow described as "peak
experience" and can remember the bliss of such
experiences. I wonder if I will ever experience that

overwhelming sense of joy and connection to the universe again. I am haunted by the turmoil of the world as well as my own inner unrest.

I recently became aware of William Sloane Coffin, a fervent pacifist, who was one of those remarkable ministers at the Riverside Church in New York. The final paragraph in his autobiography expresses what I feel:

> *So while not optimistic, I am hopeful. By this I mean that hope, as opposed to cynicism and despair, is the sole precondition for a new and better life. Realism demands pessimism. But hope demands that we take a dark view of the present only because we hold a bright view of the future; and hope arouses, as nothing else can arouse, a passion for the possible.*

Love, Ann

From: Scherr, Mary
Sent: Mon 4/10/2006 10:44 p.m.
To: ann_carli@yahoo.com
Subject: Creativity

Dear Ann,

I like the quotation from Coffin. I agree that we must have hope to arouse a passion for the possible. When I hear pessimistic judgments about human nature, I focus on Mandela's ability to forgive and promote reconciliation. Too much media coverage highlights our inhumanity. I'm committed to reading about and thinking about and observing inspiring human beings.

I also am striving to control my thoughts. Easwaran, whose meditation guidelines I try to practice, tells the following story: When elephants go down narrow lanes during festivals in India, their trunks swoop to the right and to the left and snatch up bananas or mangoes and the villagers who are selling fruit in the booths along the route can't afford that loss. But if the elephant is given a piece of bamboo, he'll put it in his trunk, hold his head high, and not steal. The mind, says Easwaran, also needs something to hold onto in meditation. When I memorize litanies or prayers and try and repeat them silently during meditation, my mind has to concentrate on the next line. It works.

In the last few letters I've shared ideas about hope, hop, and creativity. Csikszentmihalyi has studied reactions of those who transcend time and space as they are completely absorbed in their work, which is often creative. Based on my own experience, I am in what he calls "flow" whenever I'm involved in creative work. And in reflecting upon the experience, I realize I've felt a connection with the creative force of the universe. I feel, I too, have a creative small spark or core or center that I can tap into.

Early this morning I noticed my shadow was exceedingly long as I walked north along the ocean. I had not realized before that my legs were very long compared to the rest of my body. That's appropriate I thought—early in the morning I can walk long distances and feel energized by the sound and sights at the beginning of the day. As the waves receded, bubbles skated through the thin film of water—and many never broke before another wave slid upon the sand, leaving more bubbles of iridescent colors. That brief exuberant experience filled me with creative energy and joy in being alive. I was grateful for that playful gift from the sun.

Great musicians refer to the music coming through them, sculptors cut away what doesn't belong and authors describe characters creating their own story. And mystics listen to the voice within and achieve a sense of oneness with all creation.

I love to share these ideas with you… difficult though to find the right words. I'm reminded of the lines by Tukaram: "This whole vast world is but the form in which Thou showest us Thyself… What need of words?" Yet I benefit from trying to find the words!

Love, mary

From: Carli, Ann
Sent: Tues 4/11/2006 10:28 p.m.
To: Mary Scherr@aol.com
Subject: Creativity and Hope

Dear Mary,

I was introduced to Mihaly Csikszentmihalyi's
Flow at a leadership retreat in the mid-eighties and
it became an important book in my life. I was so
intrigued by his studies and theories, I tracked him
down at Claremont College and had him come
to speak at the college. I think you attended that
lecture! The elements he identifies for flow—focus,
concentration, clarity, transcending ego, present
tense, and intrinsic rather than extrinsic rewards—
seem to me to also set up peak experiences.
Perhaps they are the same, with Maslow outlining
the prerequisites and Csikszentmihalyi describing
the process. I especially valued how he explained
the tension between challenge and skills and how
flow comes when both the challenge and the skills
are high. I achieved that in my work and in my
marriage. And now both have ended.

This discussion is useful for me to think about
in terms of my emotional flat-line. I do believe
doing anything creative—from making soup to
arranging flowers to writing these letters—is a
hopeful act, a commitment to continuing on when

so much seems gone and the future, both personal and in the world sense, seems so bleak. My desire now is to move toward more creativity and regain flow in my life.

Love, Ann

From: Scherr, Mary
Sent: Wed 4/12/2006 9:22 p.m.
To: ann_carli@yahoo.com
Subject: Creativity & Complexity

Dear Ann,

You're right. I did attend that lecture by Csikszentmihalyi. So did several of my doctoral students, one of whom did research on "flow" for her doctoral dissertation. The following year I selected his *Evolving Self* as one of the texts for my Adult Development class.

Since as human beings we have evolved to the point where we can influence evolution, his views on our role in the process are significant.

The importance of choosing complexity over simplicity to promote growth is one of the central ideas I remember.

Yet complexity and simplicity, a pair of words apparently in opposition, actually are related for me. I strive to live more simply, and strive for simplicity in routines and practices so when they become habitual the processes are almost automatic and require less mental effort. Then my mental efforts to synthesize concepts, integrate experiences, and understand what it means to be fully human become increasingly complex.

I am fortunate to be able to read about and discuss with my graduate students the ideas and concepts I care most about in life. I am also fortunate to have the luxury of reflecting on these ideas. I do not need to scurry to find ways to support my children, buy meds for an ill husband, or earn money for any one of the countless needs faced by many, many women. I'm also grateful that I have the time to take long walks on the beach. For the last couple of months it has been warm enough for bare feet on the sand. And what's a beach walk without the feeling of the sand between my toes?

Love, mary

From: Carli, Ann
Sent: Mon 4/13/2006 5:29 p.m.
To: MaryScherr@aol.com
Subject: Complexity and Simplicity

Dear Mary,

It is such a struggle to find the balance between peaceful organized simplicity, which can turn into boredom, and confusing challenging complexity, which can turn into chaos.

I have long believed the answers to life are simple, but we cloud them by selfishness, ignorance, and ego. I think if we could understand our part—and responsibility—in an interrelated system we would find peace on earth and in our hearts. Several years ago I stumbled across this quote by Oliver Wendell Holmes: "I wouldn't give a fig for the simplicity on this side of complexity, but I would give my right arm for the simplicity on the far side of complexity." It felt like an epiphany that had been waiting for me to remember. It confirmed what I intuited about the profound simplicity of life, which to me is wisdom.

This past year I have been mired in a complex labyrinth. With the overlay of grief, I have wrestled with difficult house repairs, financial issues, legal problems, tax responsibilities, plus the overwhelming amount of Angelo's "collectibles."

At the beginning I couldn't fathom how I would ever manage to get rid of what filled a double storage unit plus a three-car garage. But, as all the sayings go—one step, one bite, one layer—I did accomplish it.

Did I tell you I donated 5,000 books to an organization in San Diego that gives them to prisons, hospitals, and homeless shelters? It took five truckloads to take them away. My garage is now empty. But so is my heart. If I could only find my way to the far side.

Love, Ann

From: Scherr, Mary
Sent: Tues 4/18/2006 8:06 a.m.
To: ann_carli@yahoo.com
Subject: The fugue

Dear Ann,

I'm so sorry that your heart feels empty. "Empty" is an effective word to describe one's heart, yet if it is empty it should not ache. Another paradox I suppose. As we both have found out and written about over the last year, doing something we care about, seeing friends, and keeping busy does fill the days and also the heart, at least a little. As time goes by, those same strategies (I don't like that word but can't think of a better one) are increasingly helpful, I think.

How our life journeys develop, how they differ and how they are similar have been major interests of mine for decades (including, of course, how we manage the major transitions we are discussing together in these letters).

In graduate school, I wanted to investigate the life patterns of women in a doctoral program to learn what appeared to be their developmental history. What choices did they make? What were the consequences? How did they make sense of life? I described and charted the various roles fulfilled by each of the thirty women I had interviewed. The charts noted at what age each woman became a doctoral student and/or worker, and/or wife, and/or mother. I concluded my dissertation (in 1982) with a musical metaphor for the lives of these women.

Music expresses nearly all human emotions so a musical image is appealing. The fugue emphasizes a single theme or voice and then other voices enter. The various roles a woman fulfills need to harmonize with her inner voice, her essential Self. Otherwise the roles become all consuming and she doesn't know who she really is.

Voices in a fugue can be played in different keys and different tempos analogous to a woman's roles. A minor key can be included, suggesting the ability of women to overcome tragedies and to acknowledge the realities of life.

When a woman knows her own Self and speaks her own voice her various roles can be fulfilled with integrity, unity, and complexity. And since fugues develop in a variety of complex ways, as do the lives of women, the process rather than the form is celebrated. An original and creative fugue enables a woman to strive toward who she wants to become.

During the last dozen or so years, I've discovered that meditation guides me toward a stronger sense of Self so my roles as mother, mother-in-law, grandmother, teacher and continuing student harmonize more smoothly (usually) with who I am and who I am becoming.

Did either of us ever think when we were in our thirties or forties that we'd still be thinking about who we wanted to become? I've now come to terms with the idea and actually am energized by the thought that becoming is a life long process. Becoming a more integrated Self, with less ego and more love and compassion and understanding, is a day-by-day challenge.

Considering who we are becoming may not fill empty hearts but it can certainly fill our minds with a multitude of future options. Especially when we realize we do have choices. I'm not sure these ideas are helpful, but they're ideas I am currently working on!

Love, mary

From: Carli, Ann
Sent: Thurs 4/19/2006 10:04 p.m.
To: MaryScherr@aol.com
Subject: Re: The fugue

Dear Mary,

Your metaphor of the fugue for a woman's life is
perfect! I love the image of the single voice, joined by
a second, followed by a third, a fourth, a fifth, etc., the
contrapuntal structure, the harmonics, continuous
interweaving—sometimes seeming chaotic while
having an underpinning of complicated order.
There's that complexity/simplicity again!

I am going to have to listen to the fugue in
a new way now. I wonder if the form ends by
returning to a single voice or part as our lives
have. Your statement that "music expresses nearly
all human emotions" brought to mind a favorite
quotation by Alduous Huxley, "After silence,
that which comes nearest to expressing the
inexpressible is music." As much as I love poetry,
it is music that takes my breath away, makes me
weep and sometimes even makes me believe…

Love, Ann

From: Scherr, Mary
Sent: Tues 4/21/2006 11:22 p.m.
To: ann_carli@yahoo.com
Subject: Spring

Dear Ann,

I feel a little guilty that I'm feeling joyful, even giddy when your heart has felt empty. Spring has always been my favorite season even though my sister died in spring. She was 33 and left two small boys motherless. Yet her death was calm and peaceful. She agreed with Gibran that children come through you but do not belong to you. Her serene acceptance of death and peaceful final days ushered me into a far more mature view of life with a tendency toward reflection.

With only subtle signs of the season in Southern California, spring for me is still a definite time of year. Springtime during the first two, actually three, years without Stu had moments of deep shadows but also some splashes of sun to offer hope of greater lightness. Now, once again spring is a time for adventure, romance—wild romance if only imaginary, and exuberance to mimic the profusion of buds and blooms, and an invitation to run away at least symbolically. As I write this I realize that's what I once did. I met Stu in spring, we dated less than three months, planned a wedding in three weeks, and flew to New York. I did run away—3,000 miles away from family and friends. And in 1959, a wedding between a Protestant and a Jew was considered a mixed marriage with a risky future. A challenging adventure at best.

Also my birthday comes shortly after the first day of spring. For many years I loved the fact that strawberries would be available by the end of March and I could stroll through the ranunculus fields feeling like I was in the middle of a Van Gogh painting. Now, of course, we have strawberries nearly all year long and the fields are fenced, gated, and require an admittance fee. Nevertheless, the brilliant fields are still spectacular and thousands of people visit them each year.

So… in spring I feel exuberant. My own world exudes promise, hope, and joy. Pure optimism writ large. I plan to live fully and enjoy every moment for I might only have 15 or so more springs to enjoy the magic and mystery of this world. But I am acutely aware of the staggering world problems: the growing numbers of refugees worldwide, threats to the environment, and religious, ethnic, national wars—searing realities. As I begin phased retirement, I will have more time. I want to become more passionate about social problems, compassionate about people, and take action so that I answer with my life—soon, for my lifetime is growing short.

Love, mary

From: Carli, Ann
Sent: Thurs 4/22/2006 10:04 p.m.
To: MaryScherr@aol.com
Subject: The Promise of Spring

Dear Mary,

I didn't know you had a sister who died so young. The thought of her knowing she was leaving her little children makes my heart ache— for her, for her boys, for all of you who loved her. I can see she became an important part of you. I think that as we influence each other in life, we integrate significant people in their death.

I have often thought about the legacy of my mother and my father. My strong, loving mother instilled in me courage and fierce honesty. My father, though absent and irresponsible, gave me love of language and a sense of flair. And now Angelo whispers patience, generosity, fortitude, and always, always love. I often say, "This is for you, Angelo," as I find myself rising to a challenge.

I want to give your description of and reaction to spring a title—perhaps "Hymn to Spring." My birthday follows yours in April, which I think is the most beautiful month in Southern California. I claim it entirely, celebrating my "birthmonth."

And now I buy myself birthday and anniversary presents from Angelo.

For my birthday this year, I took the train to L.A. to visit my close friend since high school. When I came home I described my experience:

Riding Backwards on the Train

I am resigned to a backward-facing seat.
Front-facing seats are filled with midriff girls,
winsome weekend couples,
fellows in a larking mood.
Everyone is moving forward except me.
Everything I see recedes.
Trees back away,
hills recoil,
telephone poles flee, wires running behind.
Crossties, once green Southern Pine,
now creased and cracked,
flash
by
like
years
in
a
retro
film.
The place I started from has vanished,
My destination will overtake me unawares.

Love, Ann

From: Scherr, Mary
Sent: Sat 4/24/2006 6:28 p.m.
To: ann_carli@yahoo.com
Subject: Eternal Spring

Dear Ann,

We originally talked about ending this correspondence after one year; however, we have continued into the spring! As our correspondence comes to its natural end, I want to share some thoughts with you. I have learned so much from your letters and I always find your poems effective. Your counseling background has enabled you to share insights as well as practical suggestions. You express your appreciation for the legacy from your mother, your father, and Angelo. But not so clear is your awareness about your own legacy—for your children, grandchildren and friends. Your strengths, values, and goodness have influenced all who have come into the orbit of your life. Consider the number of students and colleagues you have influenced.

And, in addition you are a poet who has enriched all of us fortunate enough to read your poems. (You must publish!) Your creativity continues to be reflected in your unique daily environment. I love your house, your flowers, your garden.

Perhaps most important of all, your legacy will continue with your children and your grandchildren.

When I attended a retreat with Thich Nhat Hanh that summer after Stu died, I purchased the epigram that reads: "The tears I shed yesterday have become rain." May we both continue to nourish what we value and to enhance the legacies of our husbands and our own legacies for the benefit of the next generation.

Love, mary

From: Carli, Ann
Sent: Sun 4/25/2006 9:46 p.m.
To: MaryScherr@aol.com
Subject: A Year and a Spring

Dear Mary,

We have exchanged so many words this past year—poems, quotations, meditations, lyrics to songs. Your words, without exception, have offered me ideas to reflect on and be inspired by. And your last letter touches me deeply. You are most insightful about my perceptions of my own life. I will keep your lovely positive perceptions close at hand as seeds of inspiration and encouragement to plant each spring. Meanwhile I will watch your own beautiful and loving life bloom in bountiful happiness.

I want to tell you one more story that has a song connected to it. I met Angelo when he came to California for the summer of 1957. He was twenty and I was eighteen. Were we ever eighteen? Yes, I won't forget that beautiful youthful summer with him. We had a wonderful time going to the beach, Presidio Park for picnics, Balboa Park, the Starlight Opera, the Old Globe, drive-in movies. It was idyllic. He left in September to go back to NYU and I began college at San Diego State. We agreed to write and I still have all the letters we wrote during the next two years.

The following summer I sent him this song on a 45 record. I pasted a piece of paper over the label so he had to play it to know what I was feeling. This is the song that expressed how I felt then without him and how I feel now—for the rest of my life.

They're not making the skies as blue this year
Wish you were here
As blue as they used to when you were near
Wish you were here
And the mornings don't seem as new
Brand-new as they did with you
Wish you were here
Wish you were here
Wish you were here

Someone's painting the leaves all wrong this year
Wish you were here
And why did the birds change their song this year
Wish you were here
They're not shining the stars as bright
They've stolen the joy from the night
Wish you were here
Wish you were here
Wish you were here.

Wish You Were Here   *Harold Rome*

Mary, dear friend, my children and grandchildren give me laughter and lovely moments and long-term love and support. Friends like you continue to enrich my life. I make an effort to give back to them and contribute to what Stephen Covey describes as a "circle of influence"—the people I encounter and the situations I can affect.

I also remind myself every day that the world has much greater sadness and loss than mine. So I don't feel sorry for myself. Just sorry.

Love, Ann

Suggestions

We have some suggestions for helping a grieving friend. Since suggestions are so subjective, the following list only includes suggestions that Mary and Ann found helpful.

Rather than say:

"How ARE you?"

"How are you doing?"

"Are you enjoying your retirement/the summer/ your new home?"

"What can I do?"

"Just call me if you need anything."

"You look good!"

You might say:

"It is good to see you."

"I am so glad to see you."

"You have been in my thoughts."

"I've been thinking about you."

You might volunteer to do specific tasks:

"I am going to the pharmacy/grocery store/ cleaners/post office. Do you need anything?"

"I would be glad to pick up or take houseguests to the airport."

"If you need help with plumbing/electrical/ repairs, I could help."

Rather than give:

Flowers (unless you know the person really loves and would welcome flowers)

Prepared, perishable food

You might give:

A houseplant

A gift certificate to a restaurant

A massage (if you know the person likes massages)

Movie passes

A sheet of appropriate postage stamps—graphic with birds, flowers, etc.

A box of colored file folders

Non-perishable food or gift certificate to a nearby market

An invitation to breakfast, which is casual and usually easy to schedule

Anonymously
    Take out/bring in trashcans

    Finally, do not hesitate to mention the deceased in appropriate and positive ways. Anecdotes are especially appreciated. Be sensitive to other's spiritual or religious orientation. Not everyone believes in an afterlife.

About the Authors

Ann Carli

In 2004 Ann Carli retired from a twenty-seven-year career as Dean of Arts and Letters at MiraCosta College in Oceanside, California. Prior to her career as an administrator, she taught courses in Sociology, Psychology, Women's Studies, and Communication. Her poetry has been published in Tidepools, the college literary journal.

She lives in Carlsbad where she finds flow interplaying with her grandson, creating an ever-changing garden, and rearranging words into short stories, poetry, and a novel.

Mary Woods Scherr

After teaching for twenty-one years in the Leadership Studies Doctoral Program at the University of San Diego (USD), Mary Scherr retired in 2009. Her special interests included adult development, qualitative research, and spiritual practices for leaders. Before earning her doctorate, she taught English and Women's Studies courses at MiraCosta College.

Two months before retiring from USD, she married Marvin Sippel, a recent widower with whom she shares a similar spiritual quest. They live in Carlsbad, California. Mary continues to lead retreats and meditation groups.

Made in the USA
Charleston, SC
18 February 2016